DATE DUE

			2007

The Adolescent Drug-Crime Relationship
Desistence and Gateway Theories across User Levels

Scott W. Whiteford

LFB Scholarly Publishing LLC
New York 2007

Library of Congress Cataloging-in-Publication Data

Whiteford, Scott W., 1973-
  The adolescent drug-crime relationship : desistence and gateway
theories across user levels / Scott W. Whiteford.
    p. cm. -- (Criminal justice : recent scholarship)
    Includes bibliographical references and index.
    ISBN-13: 978-1-59332-192-5 (alk. paper)
    1. Teenagers--Drug use. 2. Drug abuse and crime. 3. Criminal
behavior. I. Title.
    HV5824.Y68W495 2007
    364.36--dc22

2006035868

ISBN-10 1593321929
ISBN-13 9781593321925

Printed on acid-free 250-year-life paper.

Manufactured in the United States of America.

Table of Contents

List of Tables

List of Figures

Acknowledgements

As with any large project, a great number of individuals contributed to the completion of this book. Many colleagues deserve special recognition for their direction, advice, and time. At the University of Nebraska-Lincoln, Lynn White provided extensive guidance and helped shape the scope of this project.

At Talent Plus® several individuals contributed directly or indirectly to this manuscript. The Talent Plus® Board Members, Doug Rath, Kimberly Rath, Sandy Maxwell, and Brad Black offered encouragement and the allocation of resources. Malcolm Heard provided valuable insight and counsel throughout the journey. The Talent Plus® Research Team, Heather Wood, Sheryl Pietzyk, Stacey Dangler, Christian Wilbeck, Emily Olinger, Erica Graves, and Alyssa Hart supplied critical feedback and unlimited support.

CHAPTER 1

Introduction

According to the 2001 National Household Survey on Drug Abuse (NHSDA), 38 percent of adolescents used alcohol, marijuana, or hard drugs, and 32 percent committed crimes. Indeed, the association between drug use and crime is significant and substantial (White, Johnson, and Garrison, 1985; Fagan, Weis, and Cheng, 1990; Altschuler and Brounstein, 1991; McBride, Joe, and Simpson, 1991; Thornberry, Krohn, Lizotte, and Chard-Wierschiem, 1993; Klein, 1995; Dawkins, 1997; Flannery, Williams, and Vazsonyi, 1999; Barrera, Biglan, Ary, and Li, 2001; Bean, 2002; Welte, Barnes, Hoffman, Wieczorek, and Zhang, 2005). Focusing primarily on a cluster-analytic approach, a comprehensive examination of adolescent substance use measures will be assessed in this book. Furthermore, a comparison of the cluster analysis method to traditional substance use measures will also be utilitzed to examine the drug-crime relationship.

Using the 2001 NHSDA, a typology of the adolescent drug user through cluster analysis and alternative methods will be created to explore the link between substance use typologies and three different measures of criminal and deviant behavior using ordinary least squares regression, ordered logit regression, binary logistic regression, and multi-nomial logistic regression. This typology will also be compared to 29 alternative substance use measures found throughout the literature. With more than 17,000 adolescent reporting their substance use and criminal and deviant behavior, this data set allows for greater flexibility and statistical power than prior work.

Typology of Substance Use Patterns
A suitable measure of substance use ought to incorporate the following four ideals. First, it must include an exhaustive list of all illicit substances. Second, it must be a precise measure, which includes how much or how often substances are used over a period of time. Third, it must be a manageable measure of substance use, so it must reduce data without losing valuable information. Finally, the measure must be appropriate for use with standard analytic techniques.

Researchers confront several problems when measuring drug use. First, they must decide which drugs should be included when measuring substance use. For example, should they include tobacco and alcohol in the analysis? Tobacco and alcohol have a great deal of variance, and their statistical properties make analysis robust. Hard drug use, e.g., cocaine, lysergic acid, and heroin (Donnermeyer, 1993; Swaim, Bates, and Chavez, 1998) is so rare, however, that standard analytic techniques are less effective. In other words, by incorporating alcohol and tobacco into the drug use measure, researchers are able to use a greater number of statistics and are also able to explain more interesting findings, but they risk losing the significance of the variance contributed by the hard drug use measures.

Second, researchers must decide how to measure drug use. They can use dichotomous, ordinal-level, or ratio-level measures, but they risk collapsing hard drug users with occasional users of soft drugs (dichotomous), arbitrary cut-off levels (ordinal), or having heavily skewed data that violates standard analytic techniques (Fox, 1997), such as the assumption of continuous variance or normally distributed data (ratio). In most cases, overall drug use is so rare that researchers can basically only see whether or not the likelihood of drug use exists.

Third, researchers must decide how to combine drug use variables into an overall measure. Here, researchers can: (1) keep substance use variables as a series of individual constructs, (2) create an overall dichotomous, ordinal-level, or ratio-level variable, (3) combine the drug use variables into a sum or mean scale of substance use, or (4) create a Guttman scale. With so many options, researchers often use the simplest form of measure that is easiest to discuss. Once again, problems inundate researchers regardless of how they combine substance use measures. If they leave the variables as individual constructs, they risk measurement error, non-normally distributed data, inefficient analysis, and over-amplified models with unreliable parameter estimates (Carmines and Zeller, 1979; Tabachnick and Fidell, 1996; Kline, 1998). If they choose one overall measure, however, they risk measurement error, and these variables are weak and problematic (Carmines and Zeller, 1979; Tabachnick and Fidell, 1996; Kline, 1998). If they sum or average the substance use measures, they produce arbitrary cut-off levels for adolescent substance, which are difficult to interpret and are likely to produce a non-normal distributions. If they create a Guttman scale, which combines multiple items into a uni-dimensional variable (Devellis, 1991), they demonstrate poly-substance use but fail to distinguish particular drugs.

One under-utilized method for measuring substance use is cluster analysis. Cluster analysis allows the researcher to create a typology of adolescent substance use patterns. It assigns individuals to groups that best represent their drug use patterns (Aldenderfer and Blashfield, 1984; Nunnally and Bernstein, 1994). Cluster analysis utilizes a person-centered approach to studying substance use, which is advantageous when researching heterogeneous populations, such as substance users, and organizing them into relatively homogeneous groups (Muthen and Muthen, 2000). Using this method, the researcher retains information about the frequency of drug use and does not violate assumptions of standard analytic techniques (discussed later). The measures were multiple-item clusters with reduced error and robust parameter estimates, so they provided relatively easy analysis to complex measures.

Disadvantages to the cluster analysis method exist as well. As in most statistical practices, the researcher may manipulate the data in several different ways to create the clusters, and the clusters are not distinguished by statistical thresholds, such as, "number of times an individual used marijuana last year," which is a number that is easy to interpret. Nevertheless, cluster analysis is not as prone to data manipulation required to fit assumptions of standard analytic techniques as the arbitrary ordinal-level or dichotomous measures of adolescent substance use that are found in the literature.

The typology of substance use produced by cluster analysis is important to the field of criminology because it creates a measure that reflects accurately the breadth and depth of substance use by adolescents without violating assumptions of standard analytical techniques. An extensive search of the literature yielded no studies that focused primarily on cluster analyses to describe substance use and its correlation with criminal and deviant behavior.

The Life-course Perspective and Gateway Hypothesis
The life-course perspective and the gateway hypothesis are presented to more deeply understand the drug use typology and its link to criminal and deviant behavior.

Life-course Perspective. In developmental research, adolescents are often classified in one of two types of delinquents (or drug users), adolescence-limited and life-course-persistent (Moffitt, 1993; Moffitt, 1997). Ninety percent of youths are adolescence-limited: they commit fewer crimes and take fewer drugs than the life-course-persistent adolescent and they start delinquency later and cease earlier than life-course-persistent youths (Moffitt, 1993). The remaining 10 percent of adolescents are life-course-persistent. They start committing crimes or taking drugs in their pre-teen years, commit high rates of delinquency throughout adolescence, and are more likely to continue this pattern into their adult years (Moffitt, 1993).

Gateway Hypothesis. Derived here from the life-course perspective, the gateway hypothesis has two key assumptions. Adolescents who experiment with drugs earlier in the life-course (life-course-persistent) are more likely to use drugs more frequently than other adolescents who begin drug use later in the life-course (adolescence-limited) (Moffitt, 1993; Moffitt, 1997). Adolescent substance use begins with tobacco and alcohol, and may go through marijuana to harder drugs (Kandel, Yamaguchi, and Chen, 1992). Legal drugs, such as alcohol, are a necessary but not sufficient step to using marijuana (Kandel, 1975; Welte and Barnes, 1985). Thus, adolescents do not have to use alcohol to try marijuana.

Although the 2001 NHSDA is cross-sectional, a research question is constructed that examines some implications of both the life-course perspective and the gateway hypothesis. The results demonstrate statistical tendencies, but without longitudinal data, causal implications cannot be assessed.

Links between Adolescent Substance Use and Criminal Activity
The association between substance use and crime is strong (White, et al., 1985; Fagan, et al., 1990; Altschuler and Brounstein, 1991; McBride, et al., 1991; Thornberry, et al., 1993; Klein, 1995; Dawkins, 1997; Flannery, et al., 1999; Barrera, et al., 2001; Bean, 2002; Welte, et al., 2005), but causality, however, is difficult to determine (Fagan, et al., 1990; Altschuler and Brounstein, 1991; Bean, 2002) and is beyond the scope of this study. The goal of this study is to examine the consequences of using a cluster analysis of substance use to understand the drug-crime relationship. For this reason, a test of how drug use is associated with crime is examined.

Most studies of the link between drug use and criminal activity focused on one measure of crime. In this study, three different criminal and deviant behavior measures were used: self-reported criminal activity, self-reported criminal arrests, and criminal versatility. Using the three measures of crime, the following questions will be addressed: Are particular types of drug user significantly more likely to commit crimes, be arrested, or to be a versatile offender compared to other types of drug users or non-users?

No typology of criminal and deviant behavior will be created. The focus of this book is to examine a typology of adolescent substance use and its relationship with theoretical assumptions and crime. Creating a cluster analysis of adolescent crime is a project for a different study.

Traditional Substance Use Measures
Twenty-nine traditional measures of adolescent substance use will be created, similar to these found throughout the literature, to compare against the substance use clusters. An examination of the similarities and differences between the clusters and the traditional measures, and an introduction of two new methods of measuring traditional substance use by creating a series of nominal-level measures out of ordinal-level variables will be presented. No prior research had examined this many traditional substance use measures or introduced nominal-level measures from ordinal-level variables, which are important additions to the research on adolescent substance use.

In conclusion, the relationship between substance use and crime is a vital issue, as expressed by the volume of research dedicated to this topic and its importance for public policy. A cluster analysis on adolescent substance use will be preformed and an examination of its relationship to background variables and measures of criminal and deviant behavior will be analyzed. Next, a comparison of the traditional drug use measures to the three types of criminal and deviant behavior will be examined. Finally, 29 traditional methods of measuring drug use commonly found in the literature will be created and an analysis of how they correlate to the clusters and with the three measures of crime will be examined. Although a substantial literature finds drug use related significantly to adolescent crime, re-examining drug use with better statistical methods enables more valid conclusions about the link between adolescent substance use and criminal and deviant behavior.

CHAPTER 2
Treacherous Measurements

Researchers face difficulties when conceptualizing adolescent drug use, and they disagree as to the best way to measure it. Although many adolescents report abstaining from substances or using only a few substances, drug use ought to be conceptualized to include the breadth and extent of illicit substance use by individuals. It ought to assess the number of substances used as well as the frequency and amount of each substance used because researchers need to understand the differences among drug users and their relationship to other social phenomena. Aside from concerns regarding validity, freedom from bias, and reliability (all of which are addressed later in this book), a good measure of drug use should: include a representative list of all illicit drugs, include a precise measure of each drug, reduce data without losing valuable information, and be applicable to standard analytic techniques. In this section, four aspects of a good measure of substance use, a review of how prior researchers constructed substance use, and an overview of the cluster-analytic method will be presented.

Desirable Properties of a Drug Use Measure
An Exhaustive List of Substances. To understand differences among substance users, and to explore their relationship to other social phenomena, researchers need to include an exhaustive list of all illicit substances when

measuring adolescent drug use because failure to do so may relegate the construct as invalid. They face several dilemmas, however, when deciding how to operationalize an exhaustive measure of drug use. The 2001 NHSDA reports that adolescents use over 100 different drugs, so it may be difficult for researchers to include all of these drugs in a measure of substance use. Therefore, an exhaustive measure of adolescent substance use is difficult to construct. However, by using the cluster analysis method, 12 types of substances will be integrated into a single construct, which includes virtually every illicit drug. In other work, pain relievers includes Oxycontin and codiene.

Another dilemma is that adolescents drink alcohol and ingest tobacco more frequently than other substances. Including these substances in an overall measure of drug use may produce misleading results because of their substantial variance. In other words, alcohol and tobacco may overwhelm the other drugs statistically, and it may be difficult for researchers to get and accurate gage of the overall drug use impact. Alcohol and tobacco both have legal ages of consumption; tobacco is 18 and alcohol is 21. Tobacco may be easily available to adolescents in this study whose peers are of legal age, but alcohol is not because the legal age for alcohol consumption is three years greater than tobacco. Therefore, alcohol—but not tobacco—will be included in the measure of substance use presented in this study.

A Precise Measure of Substance Use. Researchers must choose a measure that incorporates both breadth and depth of adolescent substance use. A precise measure includes how much or how often the individual uses substances over a period of time. This measure must also include how much they use on each occasion. The cluster analysis method allows reserachers to maintain ratio-level data for all of the drugs used in the analysis.

A Manageable Measure of Substance Use. Researchers must reduce the number of substance use variables in their analysis to a manageable number of drug use measures or scales. Leaving them as multiple individual measures will increase the number of degrees of freedom needed for analysis, which in small samples may create unreliable parameter estimates (Tabachnick and Fidell, 1996). Collapsing multiple drug use variables into a single variable, however, may lead to the loss of valuable information. Therefore, a method that collapses data without creating unreliable parameter estimates or losing valuable information is critical. Cluster analysis is a person-centered method (Muthen and Muthen, 2000), which allows the researcher to incorporate all of the substances by grouping individuals and, therefore, may minimize the loss of valuable information.

Substance Use Measures and Standard Analytical Techniques. Researchers must create their measures of adolescent substance use so that the measures may be used in standard analytical techniques. Most standard analytical techniques rely on various assumptions about the data, such as the assumptions of a normal distribution and continuous data (Fox, 1997). Most researchers violate at least one of these assumptions when creating their drug use measures because the variance within their measures of substance use often is skewed. In other words, most statistical techniques have many rules that researchers must follow, but because most adolescents do not use substances, the statistics become more unstable. However, cluster analysis creates a series of nominal-level groups that can be used in standard analytical techniques.

Using the cluster analysis method may be the most appropriate technique for analyzing adolescent substance use. It allows the researcher to use ratio-level measures without losing data or creating arbitrary cut-off points. It groups a complete range of substances, so the analytical models are not incomplete, and it groups individuals based on their substance use patterns, so it does not violate assumptions of standard analytical techniques.

Which Drugs Should Be Measured?
The first step of operationalizing substance use is for the researcher to choose which drugs to include in the analysis. Several researchers included alcohol or tobacco in their measures of drug use (Marcos, Bahr, and Johnson, 1986; Hundleby and Mercer, 1987; Cochran and Akers, 1989; Brownfield and Sorenson, 1991; McGee, 1992; Kinnier, Metha, Okey, and Keim, 1994; Duncan, Tildesly, Duncan, and Hops, 1995; Harrison, Fulkerson, and Beebe, 1997; Novins and Mitchell, 1998; Flannery, et al., 1999; Keller, Catalano, Haggerty, and Fleming, 2002; Kelly, Comello, and Hunn, 2002). One advantage of including alcohol and tobacco in an overall measure of substance use was that these measures have substantial variance because adolescents use these drugs more regularly than harder substances, and as a result, these measures were robust. The 2001 NHSDA reported that adolescents drank alcohol and ingested tobacco four times more often than any other substance. A disadvantage was content validity, which is the evaluation of the measurement as it reflects a specific phenomenon in society (Carmines and Zeller, 1979). Alcohol and tobacco may overwhelm hard drugs in an overall measure because of their substantial variance. By including them in an overall measure of substance use, the

researcher insinuates that alcohol and tobacco are similar to hard drugs. Therefore, the researcher has to determine whether including alcohol and tobacco yields an appropriate measure of drug use.

Several researchers excluded tobacco and alcohol in their measures of adolescent substance use or included them as separate measures (Wechsler and Thum, 1973; Akers and Cochran, 1985; White, et al., 1985; Downs and Robertson, 1990; Smart, et al., 1990; Donnermeyer, 1993; Stice, Barrera, and Chassin, 1993; Benda, 1995; Havey and Dodd, 1995; Parker, Weaver, and Calhoun, 1995; Stice and Barrera, 1995; Wood, Cochran, Pfefferbaum, and Arneklev, 1995; Graham, 1996; Andrews, Hops, and Duncan, 1997; Bahr, Maughan, Marcos, and Li, 1998; Ellickson, Bui, Bell, and McGuigan, 1998; Diego, et al., 2003). By keeping alcohol and tobacco separate, these approaches had stronger content validity than those including alcohol and tobacco in an overall measure of substance use.

A substantial problem occurred for researchers who separated substance use measures from tobacco and alcohol, however, because adolescents used hard drugs so infrequently that variance was minimal (Hundleby and Mercer, 1987; Stice, et al., 1993; Keller, et al., 2002). In fact, Hundleby and Mercer (1987) included only measures of tobacco, alcohol, and marijuana because measures of hard drugs did not have enough variance to be included in their model. For this book, hard drugs were defined as substances other than alcohol, tobacco, and marijuana (Donnermeyer, 1993; Swaim, et al., 1998). Lack of variance was a major concern because differences among varying types of substance users may not be detected. Researchers can overcome this problem by over-sampling those who have used hard substances or using a large representative survey where a greater number of adolescents have used hard drugs. In other words, by finding adolescents who use substances and interviewing them at a higher rate, researchers can find most robust statistical properties. However, the results cannot be generalized to the population because the sample is no longer representative.

Finally, some researchers did not disclose how they measured adolescent substance use (Lempers, Clark-Lempers, and Simons, 1989; Miller-Johnson, Loehman, Core, Terry, and Hyman, 1998). Without presenting their drug use measures, their conclusions are suspect.

How Should Drug Use Be Measured?
Most research presented in the literature relied on regression, or forms of regression, as the primary analytic method, which is probably the most popular and least complicated statistic to analyze substance use. For regression analysis to yield proper results, data should have a normal distribution and normal variance. A nominal distribution means that the frequency of use ought to look similar to a bell-shaped curve if charted on graphing paper. In other words, if "0" use (never) was minimum and "10" use (everyday) was maximum, then "0" and "10" would be very short, whereas "5" and "6" would be at the zenith. Substance use patterns do not follows this statistical distribution. Continuous vaiance implies that no disruption in the pattern of frequencies exist. In other words, at least one respondent has "0" use, at least one has "1" use, at least another has "2" use, and so on until the frequency chain is broken.

Regression Assumption of a Normal Distribution. The normal distribution assumption states that, within reason, individuals are normally distributed among the possible responses (Lewis-Beck, 1980; Darlington, 1990). Frequency of drug use among adolescents is not normally distributed. If the possible responses range from zero (never use) to 365 (use every day), then the respondents typically will cluster around zero, one, or two, with a few scattered throughout the rest of the range. On a graph, with number of individuals on the Y-axis and possible responses on the X-axis, the line will resemble a ski slope, with most individuals clustered to the left of the graph. This type of measure is positively skewed. Although minor skew is acceptable (Tabachnick and Fidell, 1996), this type of skew is severe and unacceptable.

Regression Assumption of Continuous Variance. Standard analytical techniques assume continuous variables, especially for the dependent variable (Fox, 1997). In a ratio-level variable, if many of the individuals cluster around zero, one, or two, with gaps between greater numbers, this assumption is violated.

A solution to the violation of this assumption is to Winsorize the respondents (Hoaglin, Mosteller, and Tukey, 1983). In this case, the researcher maintains response order but eliminates gaps in the sequence by dropping unused responses. In other words, if several respondents state they used cocaine 15 days out of the past year, and a few state they used cocaine 18 days, but nobody states they used 16 or 17, Winsorizing eliminates the gap between 15 and 18 by changing the responses of those who said 18 to 16, thereby maintaining order but eliminating gaps. Winsorizing eliminates violating the assumption of continual variance for substance use measures, but the measure still violates the assumption of normality.

Researchers have several other options when measuring substance use. Dichotomous measures, ordinal measures, ratio measures, and qualitative data will be examined in this study.

Dichotomous Measures. Some researchers chose the most basic option of operationalizing substance use, which was to dichotomize their responses (Wechsler and Thum, 1973; Brownfield and Sorenson, 1991; Parker, et al., 1995; Wood, et al., 1995; Graham, 1996; Andrews, et al., 1997; Harrison, et al., 1997; Novins and Mitchell, 1998; Keller, et al., 2002). Those individuals who had never used the substance were coded zero, and those individuals who had at least tried the substance were coded one. Neither assumption is violated, but content validity is a problem because individuals who have merely tried the drug were coded the same as individuals who used the drug habitually.

Ordinal Measures. Some researchers chose to operationalize drug use with a ordinal-level measures (Wilsnack and Wilsnack, 1980; Akers and Cochran, 1985; White, et al., 1985; Marcos, et al., 1986; Hundleby and Mercer, 1987; Cochran and Akers, 1989; Smart, et al., 1990; Cochran, et al., 1993; Donnermeyer, 1993; Stice, et al., 1993; Kinnier, et al., 1994; Benda, 1995; Duncan, et al., 1995; Havey and Dodd, 1995; Stice and Barrera, 1995; Osgood, Wilson, O'Malley, Bachman, and Johnston, 1996; Youniss, Yates, and Su, 1997; Ellickson, et al., 1998; Bensley, Southwick, Spieker, van Eenwyk, and Schoder, 1999; Flannery, et al., 1999; Parker, Calhoun, and Weaver, 2000; Kelly, et al., 2002; Diego, et al., 2003). In this case, the researcher had to choose which levels to include. For instance, Donnermeyer (1993) coded no drug use as zero, drug use of less than once a month as one, between once a month and once a week as two, between once a week and three times a week as three, and more than three times a week as four. In this case, researchers retained more information than when dichotomizing the responses, but the cut-offs were arbitrary, heavy users were still grouped with occasional users, and the assumption of normality was still violated.

Ratio Measures. Another possibility for measuring substance use was to maintain the original ratio measures of frequency (Downs and Robertson, 1990; McGee, 1992; Bahr, et al., 1998; Welte, et al., 2001). This method produces a skewed measure, however, because most hard drug use is only occasional. McGee (1992) counted only alcohol and marijuana in her measure of substance use because of this problem. Although this method retains the most information about quantity, it violates the two assumptions mentioned above, possibly biasing the results (Lewis-Beck, 1980; Fox, 1997).

Qualitative Data. Another method for measuring drug use was to use qualitative data (Swaim, et al., 1998). Qualitative researchers use nonparametric data collection samples. Examples of qualitative data are ethnographies—where the researchers live covertly with their subjects—and non-paramtrics samples, such as snowball samples, where the researchers conduct in-depth interviews. Although these samples are rich in information, they do not provide an aggregate picture of incidence and prevalence, so researchers using this method cannot generalize their findings to the population.

Should Different Drugs Be Combined into Overall Measures?

After deciding which measures are most appropriate, researchers are confronted with the choice of how to introduce the measures into a single construct or several different constructs. Four methods of constructing measures of substance use appear in the literature: (1) leaving them as individual measures, (2) using one overall dichotomized or ordinal measure, (3) summing or averaging the measures, or (4) combining the measures into a Guttman Scale.

Several Individual Measures. Some researchers kept the measures of adolescent substance use as individual constructs (Wechsler and Thum, 1973; Hundleby and Mercer, 1987; McGee, 1992; Donnermeyer, 1993; Benda, 1995; Havey and Dodd, 1995; Graham, 1996; Andrews, et al., 1997; Bahr, et al., 1998; Ellickson, et al., 1998; Diego, et al., 2003). All of the measures remained single-item indicators, but this method raises the problem of measurement error (Carmines and Zeller, 1979), lack of statistical power (Tabachnick and Fidell, 1996), and greater risk of a false positive or Type I error (Kline, 1998).

Compounding the problem of using several individuals constructs, the literature was inconsistent as to which drugs to include in the analyses. For example, Diego and associates (2003) used measures of cigarette use, alcohol use, marijuana use, and cocaine use. Bahr and associates (1998) used measures of alcohol, marijuana, and depressants. Weschler and Thum (1973) included amphetamines, barbiturates, cough syrup, glue sniffing, heroin, LSD, and marijuana. Incorporating many variables into a single analysis increases the degrees of freedom needed, and the effect on the parameter estimates may lead to unstable results (Tabachnick and Fidell, 1996).

Overall Dichotomous, Ordinal-Level, or Ratio-Level Measures. A substantial literature used an overall single-item indicator of substance use at the dichotomous-level, usually user versus non-user (Novins and Mitchell, 1998; Keller, et al., 2002), ordinal-level (Akers and Cochran, 1985; Cochran and Akers, 1989; Smart, et al., 1990), or ratio-level (Welte, et al., 2001). The overall ordinal-level and ratio-level measures capture depth of substance use, but not breadth of use, because individuals who habitually use one drug may be in the highest level of substance use. Unfortunately, these measures could not differentiate among individuals who used a variety of different drugs, but whose overall drug use was infrequent, such as an individual who has once tried alcohol, marijuana, and cocaine.

Multiple-item indicators, however, have advantages compared to single-item indicators. First, multiple-item indicators increase validity by covering the entire dimension of a construct (Carmines and Zeller, 1979). They also decrease random error (as when researchers enter data incorrectly or code individuals non-uniformly) (Carmines and Zeller, 1979). Multiple-item indicators increase precision because they have greater variance, making it easier to rank respondents. They allow researchers to evaluate reliability through inter-item analysis, such as Cronbach's Alpha (McIver and Carmines, 1981; Carmines and Zeller, 1979). Finally, multiple-item indicators allow for greater degrees of freedom in multi-variate models. When a model has many indicators, it must have a large sample to allow for a greater number of degrees of freedom. If the researcher uses a small sample and a model with many indicators, they will have unreliable parameter estimates (Tabachnick and Fidell, 1996). For example, if researchers uses a multitude of single-item indicators, one to represent each drug, parameter estimates may be unreliable and unpredictable findings.

Sum   or   Mean   Measures.   Some   researchers dichotomized each individual measure of substance use and then   summed   or   averaged   the   dichotomized   measures (Parker, et al., 1995).   Thus, if eight drugs existed in the measure,   the   possible   responses   were   zero   to   eight. Usually, this method violates the assumption of normality and content validity.   For example, individuals who uses methamphetamines every day but rarely used other drugs will be coded a one or two.   Individuals who have merely tried marijuana, cocaine, and heroin will be coded a three. This measure works well to analyze poly-substance use but fails to evaluate frequency of use.

Other   researchers   summed   or   averaged   ordinal-   or ratio-level measures of substance use (White, et al., 1985; Marcos, et al., 1986; Downs and Robertson, 1990; Stice, et al., 1993; Kinnier, et al., 1994; Duncan, et al., 1995; Stice and Barrera, 1995; Harrison, et al., 1997; Flannery, et al., 1999; Kelly, et al., 2002).   This   practice   violates   the assumption   of   normality   and   probably   the   continuous variable assumption, as well   For example, Kinnier and associates (1994) summed 27 ordinal measures of drugs. Each individual measure contained seven ordinal levels. By   summing   these   variables,   Kinnier   and   associates' (1994) substance use measure had a range of 27 to 189. The measure was probably skewed and probably did not have continuous variance.

Guttman   Scale.   Finally, a small literature used a Guttman-type   Scale   (Brownfield   and   Sorenson,   1991;

Chapple, Hope, and Whiteford, 2005) to measure drug use. Guttman scales are multiple-item measures combined into a uni-dimensional, single-item scale (DeVellis, 1991). Chapple and associates (2005) used an ordinal-level, single-item, integrated indicator to measure drug use. Adolescents who did not use drugs were coded zero. Adolescents who used only alcohol were coded one. Adolescents who used only marijuana were coded two. Adolescents who used alcohol and marijuana were coded three. Adolescents who used alcohol, marijuana, and hard drugs were coded four. This measure captured poly-substance use, but it failed to differentiate users who chronically used a few substances.

In conclusion, throughout the literature, researchers operationalized substance use in the following seven methods: (1) a series of dichotomous measures of individual substances, (2) a series of ordinal-level measures of individual substances, (3) an overall dichotomous substance use measure, (4) an overall ordinal-level substance use measure, (5) the sum or average of dichotomous measures of substance use, (6) the sum or average of ordinal-level measures substance use, or (7) a Guttman-type scale of substance use. All of these traditional measures will be analyzed in Chapter 6.

Cluster Analysis
What is the best measure of adolescent substance use? An underutilized method is cluster analysis, which may be the most appropriate method of measuring adolescent drug use. Cluster analysis is a statistical procedure that categorizes a sample of heterogeneous individuals into relatively homogeneous groups based on variables in a particular data set (Muthen and Muthen, 2000). It is most appropriate

when the researcher intends to create a typology of individuals (Aldenderfer and Blashfield, 1984). According to Aldenderfer and Blashfield (1984), the cluster analysis method consists of five steps. The researcher must (1) pick a data set, (2) define a group of variables to be used in the cluster analysis, (3) compute the similarities among the entities (substance use), (4) use a cluster analysis method to create the clusters, and (5) validate the findings in the cluster solution. To best analyze the data, frequency of use variables that measure adolescent use of 12 substance use measures from the 2001 National Household Study on Drug Abuse was included and Ward's method of cluster analysis was implemented.

Cluster analysis allows the researcher to create an empirical typology of adolescent substance use patterns. It assigns individuals into classifications that best represent their drug use patterns based on meaningful latent groups (Nunnally and Bernstein, 1994; Muthen and Muthen, 2000). It can distinguish among individuals who, in other methods, would have received the same score, for instance:

- an individual who consumes alcohol regularly, smokes marijuana on occasion, and has tried cocaine.

- an individual who consumes alcohol infrequently, has rarely used marijuana, but uses methamphetamines regularly.

- an individual who consumes alcohol frequently, smokes marijuana regularly, and uses many hard drugs.

Most researchers found significant relationships between drug use and criminal and deviant behavior (White, et al., 1985; Fagan, et al., 1990; Altschuler and Brounstein, 1991; McBride, et al., 1991; Thornberry, et al., 1993; Klein, 1995; Dawkins, 1997; Flannery, et al., 1999; Barrera, et al., 2001; Bean, 2002), but their measures may have violated standard analytical technique assumptions and could not distinguish among different types of hard drug users. Cluster analysis does not violate the assumption of normality because the cluster creates groups, and groups are a nominal measure. It does not violate the assumption of continuous variance because each group has at least one respondent. The overwhelming advantages to the cluster analysis method are that the measure is holistic, all relevant information is used, and content validity is maintained.

The cluster analysis method has shortcomings as well. Visual inspection of the data, rather than statistical procedures, divides the adolescents into groups. Additionally, four methods to produce clusters exist, Ward's method, average linkage, complete linkage, and single linkage, and the four different methods may yield different results (Aldenderfer and Blashfield, 1984). Regardless of its shortcomings, cluster analysis may be the most appropriate method of measuring adolescent substance use.

CHAPTER 3

Studying Drugs and Crime

Cluster analysis is primarily an empirical comparison of drug use measures, but it is important to implement theory to frame the research questions. Therefore, the versatility assumption of delinquent behavior, the life-course perspective, and the gateway hypothesis (derived from the life-course perspective) will all be examined, as they relate to adolescent drug use and criminal and deviant behavior.

Versatility Assumption

The versatility assumption states that adolescents who commit crimes or take drugs do not specialize in one type of crime or drug (Klein, 1984; Britt, 1994). Labeled as cafeteria-style delinquency, Malcolm Klein (1984) found that 21 of 33 subjects involved in criminal activity were versatile in their criminal behavior (Klein 1984). Similarly, using the Seattle Youth Survey, Britt (1994) found that criminals showed little evidence of specialization, although criminals did specialize if they found a crime that they did well (Britt 1994). Furthermore, Gottfredson and Hirschi (1990) found an overlap between crimes and legal—but risky—behaviors.

The use of the versatility assumption in this research is twofold. First, the drug use clusters for a versatility of drug use will be examined. In other words, do certain drug use clusters demonstrate versatility in adolescent drug use patterns? Furthermore, will all 12 drug use measures be represented in some, or all, of the adolescent drug use groups? Second, a measure of criminal versatility will be created to examine whether certain groups of drug users are versatile in their criminal offending.

Life-course Perspective and Gateway Hypothesis

It is important to incorporate the life-course perspective as it relates to adolescent substance use to have a more holistic understanding of the transitions of adolescent substance use. Throughout the population, criminal behavior begins early in adolescence, peaks at 17 (Hirschi and Gottfredson, 1983; Blumstein and Cohen, 1987; Sampson and Laub, 2003) or 18 (Warr, 1993) years of age, and declines throughout the 20s. Adolescent drug use patterns follow a similar path but peak at 25 and decline more slowly than criminal behavior (Bean, 2002).

Early social environment is important in determining criminal and deviant behavior and drug use (Hirschi, 1969; Hirschi and Gottfredson, 1983). Developing strong bonds to social institutions, such as the family (Hirschi, 1969; Gottfredson and Hirschi, 1990), helps determine whether youths become non-users, adolescence-limited, or life-course-persistent individuals (Moffitt, 1993; Moffitt, 1997).

In the pre-teen years, adolescents substance users fall into two types of individuals (Moffitt, 1993). The majority of adolescent drug users fall under the category of adolescence-limited delinquents whose involvement in crime and drug use is temporary (Moffitt, 1993). These adolescents follow the typical age-crime and age-drug curves, and they may experience periods of their adolescence where they are crime and drug free. A few adolescents warrant the term life-course-persistent. They begin offending or using drugs early in the life-course and desist from crime and drugs later than other adolescents (Moffitt, 1993). Life-course-persistent delinquents begin their criminal behavior and drug use earlier, commit more crime, use more drugs, and desist later than most adolescents (Moffitt, 1993). Fewer than 10 percent of all adolescents merit this label (Moffitt, 1993).

The gateway hypothesis is drawn from life-course perspective. Adolescents who use drugs earlier in the life-course are more likely to demonstrate a greater depth and breadth of drug use than other adolescents. They fit Moffitt's (1993, 1997) notion of adolescence-limited and life-course-persistent drug use. Adolescents who start drinking alcohol at a young age are more likely to experiment with a greater number of drugs, and use drugs more frequently, than youths who start drug use later in their adolescent years.

Additionally, adolescent drug use follows a specific path through licit drugs to illicit drugs. First stated as a "stepping stone" theory by the Federal Bureau of Investigation in 1965 (Welte and Barnes, 1985), this theory posits that adolescents use alcohol, graduate to marijuana, and eventually to hard drugs, such as heroin (Kandel, 1975; Kandel, et al., 1992). Adult legal drugs, such as alcohol, are a necessary—but not sufficient—step to using marijuana (Kandel, 1975; Welte and Barnes, 1985). Therefore, along with tobacco, alcohol is the gateway drug for adolescents (Kandel, et al., 1992).

In support of the gateway hypothesis, researchers found that only one-tenth of one percent of adolescents who used hard drugs did not previously use alcohol (Welte and Barnes 1985), and only two to three percent of adolescents who used hard drugs did not use marijuana (Kandel, 1975). Using longitudinal data, Kandel (1975) found a definite pattern from alcohol (and cigarettes) through marijuana use to other illicit drugs. Furthermore, the majority of youths who used alcohol or marijuana never progress to harder drugs (2001 NHSDA).

Using the 2001 NHSDA, both paths of the gateway hypothesis will be examined. First, derived from life-course perspective, a hypothesis that a small number of adolescents will use drugs more frequently and use harder substances than the majority of adolescents will be presented. Second, adolescent substance use patterns across the ages of 12 through 17 will be explored, and the expected findings are that no substance use and alcohol use will be highest for young adolescents and marijuana and hard drug use will be highest for older adolescents. Due to the limitations of the 2001 NHSDA, this will be a cross-sectional examination of associations implied by the gateway hypothesis.

Prior Empirical Work

Two sets of prior will work will be reviewed. First prior work as it relates to the predictors of adolescent substance use and adolescent crime and deviance will be examined; second, adolescent substance use as a correlate of adolescent delinquency will be explored. The versatility assumption implies those variables that predict substance use are likely to predict crime and delinquency as well.

Predictors of Adolescent Substance Use

Most studies of adolescent substance use controlled for a least one of the following: age, gender, race, and class. Older adolescents were more likely than younger adolescents to use alcohol (Cochran, 1993; Benda, 1995; Duncan, et al., 1995; Wood, et al., 1995; Bahr, et al., 1998;

Parker, et al., 2000; Ford, 2005), marijuana (Benda, 1995; Duncan, et al., 1995; Wood, et al., 1995; Andrews, et al., 1997; Bahr, et al., 1998; Akers and Lee, 1998), and hard drugs (White, et al., 1985; Duncan, et al., 1995; Stice and Barrera, 1995; Bahr, et al., 1998; Goode, 2001; Keller, et al., 2002), although Benda (1995) found no age relationship with hard drug use (amphetamines). Overall, substance use peaked at age 25 (Bean, 2002).

The literature was inconsistent in its analysis of gender and substance use. Some researchers stated that girls started drinking at younger ages than boys but increased use less rapidly over time (Duncan, et al., 1995), but other researchers found that boys started drinking earlier in the life-course than girls (Weschler and Thum, 1973; Donnermeyer, 1993; Bensley, et al., 1999). Boys drank more and more often (Wilsnack and Wilsnack, 1980; Cochran, 1993; Benda, 1995; Bensley, et al., 1999; Parker, et al., 2000) and used substances more often than girls, regardless of drug choice (Duncan, et al., 1995; Osgood, et al., 1996). Simons-Morton and Chen (2006) found that boys start using substance earlier than girls, but girls increased use more quickly over time than did boys. Donnermeyer (1993), however, found that boys did not start using marijuana or hard drugs earlier in the life-course than girls, and other researchers found no gender differential in substance use (Benda, 1995; Parker, et al., 1995; Stice and Barrera, 1995; Wood, et al., 1995; Andrews, et al., 1997; Keller, et al., 2002; Ford, 2005).

Class status did not predict adolescent substance use (Arafat, 1979; Hundleby and Mercer, 1987 McGee, 1992; Benda, 1995; Parker, et al., 1995). For example, individuals of all classes were equally likely to use alcohol (Arafat, 1979; Hundleby and Mercer, 1987; Benda, 1995), marijuana (Hundleby and Mercer, 1987; McGee, 1992; Benda, 1995), or hard drugs (Benda, 1995; Parker, et al., 1995), except for wine, which was positively correlated with socio-economic status (Cochran, 1993). Sudden economic hardship, however, was indirectly predictive of adolescent delinquency and substance use (Lempers and et al., 1989).

Finally, the correlation between adolescent substance use and race varied within the literature. Researchers found that non-Hispanic whites (Benda, 1995; Parker, et al., 1995; Wood, et al., 1995; Graham, 1996), Native Americans (Wood, et al., 1995; Novins and Mitchell, 1998), and Hispanics (Sokol-Katz, Dunham, and Zimmerman, 1997; Flannerly, et al., 1999) were more likely to use substances than individuals of other races. In fact, non-Hispanic whites reported drinking more on each occasion and drinking more often than African-Americans (Brown, Parks, Zimmerman, and Phillips, 1993; Cochran, 1993). However, other researchers found no racial differences (Ford, 2005). When controlling for other factors, African-Americans were significantly less likely to smoke, drink alcohol, and use hard drugs than were non-Hispanic whites (Wood, et al., 1995; Sokol-Katz, et al., 1997).

Predictors of Adolescent Crime and Deviance
The literature that examined age, gender, race, and class as predictors of adolescent crime and delinquency was consistent. Older adolescents were more likely to commit nearly every type of crime as compared to younger adolescents (Hirschi and Gottfredson, 1983; Blumstein and Cohen, 1987; Warr, 1993; Beyers and Loeber, 2003), especially boys (White, et al., 1985). The exception was violent crime, where no difference existed (Heimer, 1997;

Matsueda and Heimer, 1997). As they aged, boys increased their delinquent activities faster than girls, implying a quadratic effect (White, et al., 1985). As adolescents aged, however, they decreased their versatility in crime (Beyers and Loeber, 2003). Crime peaked at age 17 (Hirschi and Gottfredson, 1983; Blumstein and Cohen, 1987; Sampson and Laub, 2003) or 18 (Warr, 1993).

A substantial literature found that boys were more likely than girls to commit violent and personal crimes (Hindelang, 1979; Thompson, Mitchell, and Dodder, 1984; Osgood, et al., 1996; Sokol-Katz, et al., 1997). In fact, Hindelang (1979) found that at least 80 percent of all rapes, robberies, aggravated assaults, simple assaults, car thefts, and larcenies were committed by males. The literature was inconsistent about gender and property crimes and minor offenses. Widom (1989) found that girls were more likely than boys to commit property and order offenses, such as loitering, disorderly conduct, and curfew violations. Some researchers, however, found that boys were more likely than girls to commit minor crimes (Hindelang, 1979; Benda, 1995; Sokol-Katz, et al., 1997) or property offenses (Hindelang, 1979; Thompson, et al., 1984; Benda, 1995; Osgood, et al., 1996; Sokol-Katz, et al., 1997), and other researchers found no gender differences in property or status offenses (Benda, 1995).

In their classic study of Chicago, Shaw and McKay (1942) found class, not race, was a predictor of adolescent delinquency. Other researchers also found that lower socio-economic status was significantly correlated with delinquency, especially property (Matsueda and Heimer, 1997), personal (Benda, 1995; Matsueda and Heimer, 1997) and serious and violent crimes (Heimer, 1997; Matsueda and Heimer, 1997). Sudden economic hardship was related indirectly to criminal and deviant behavior among adolescents as well (Lempers, et al., 1989).

As for race and ethnicity, Hispanics (Sokol-Katz, et al., 1997; Flannerly, et al., 1999) and African-Americans (Blumstein and Cohen, 1987; Sommers and Baskin, 1993; Sokol-Katz, et al., 1997) were significantly more likely to commit minor and serious delinquency than non-Hispanic whites. Other researchers, however, found no significant difference between non-Hispanic whites and African-Americans on violent (Heimer, 1997; Matsueda and Heimer 1997), person, property, or status crimes (Benda, 1995). The literature suggested that non-Hispanic whites start offending at an older age than adolescents of other races (Hirschi and Gottfredson, 1983).

Drugs and Crime
The association between adolescent substance use and criminal and deviant behavior is significant and substantial (White, et al., 1985; Fagan, et al., 1990; Altschuler and Brounstein, 1991; McBride, et al., 1991; Thornberry, et al., 1993; Klein, 1995; Dawkins, 1997; Flannery, et al., 1999; Barrera, et al., 2001; Welte, et al., 2001; Bean, 2002). Although the causal process is unclear (Fagan, et al., 1990; Altschuler and Brounstein, 1991; Bean, 2002; Welte, et al, 2005), researchers found that adolescents who used alcohol, marijuana, and hard drugs were significantly more likely to be involved in delinquency. Welte and associates (2001), however, in their longitudinal study of cross-lagged effects, found that substance use and crime rarely influenced each other when other demographic variables were held constant. Altschuler and Brounstein (1991) found that adolescents rarely commit crimes while high on drugs, and most juveniles did not commit crimes to obtain

drugs. Conversely, Bean (2002) found that drug users needed money to support habits, and the drugs caused users to behave in bizarre and destructive manners. Burglary, followed by drug sales, was the most common type of crime committed while high on drugs (Altschuler and Brounstein, 1991).

Fagan and associates (1990) dissected the drugs-crime relationship and found that more serious offenders used drugs and alcohol more frequently. Frequency of use of a particular substance increased with severity of delinquency, but poly-substance use varied little with increased delinquency. Adolescents who used a particular substance frequently, rather than multiple substances less frequently, were more likely to be involved in crime and deviance. The frequency of getting high was not related to the frequency of committing crimes but to the increasing severity of the crime (Fagan, et al., 1990).

In an examination of 21 different types of crimes, Dawkins (1997) found that alcohol was most strongly associated with poly-criminal activity. Twenty of the 21 crimes were associated with alcohol. Eleven of the 21 crimes were associated with marijuana. Twelve were associated with heroin. For neither marijuana use nor heroin use did a particular pattern of specialty in criminal behavior emerge. Therefore, for all three drugs, versatility in criminal offending appeared to exist.

Demographic differences between adolescent drug use and crime existed as well. Drug use peaks at the age of 25 (Bean, 2002), while crime and deviance peaked at seventeen (Hirschi and Gottfredson, 1983) or eighteen (Warr, 1993). White and associates (1985) found that alcohol, marijuana, and hard drug use were related to minor crimes (petty larceny and vandalism) and property crimes (grand larceny and breaking and entering) for boys. For violent crimes (assault), however, alcohol was the driving force for 18 year-olds, while marijuana and hard substances were the link for 15 year-olds. For girls, no relationship existed between alcohol, marijuana, and hard drug use and property or violent crime, but one did exist between substance use of all types and minor crimes (White, et al., 1985).

Overall, older adolescents were more likely than younger ones to use drugs and commit crimes. Boys were more likely than girls to use drugs and commit crimes, except for property crimes. No differences existed between adolescents who received income subsidies and those who did not and their drug use patterns, but adolescents of lower socio-economic classes were more likely than others to commit crimes. Non-Hispanic whites were more likely than adolescents of other races to use drugs but less likely to commit crimes. Not surprisingly, adolescents substance use and criminal and deviant behavior was positively correlated.

Statement of the Problem
A thorough search of the literature did not yield a study that used cluster analysis to analyze adolescent drug use as it relates to criminal and deviant behavior. Therefore, cluster analysis is used to examine adolescent substance use and correlate it to three measures of crime. Alternative, or traditional, substance use variables similar to those found in the literature will be created as well, to compare with the cluster analysis groups. Finally, the traditional measures of drug use with the three measures of crime will be examined.

Six questions will be analyzed in this study, presented here in Figure 1. Age, gender, race, and income subsidies are the four control variables that shall be referred to as the background variables. The adolescent substance use variable is a series of traditional measures found throughout the literature and a series of groups created by cluster analysis. The adolescent criminal activity, criminal arrests, and criminal versatility measures are all endogenous variables.

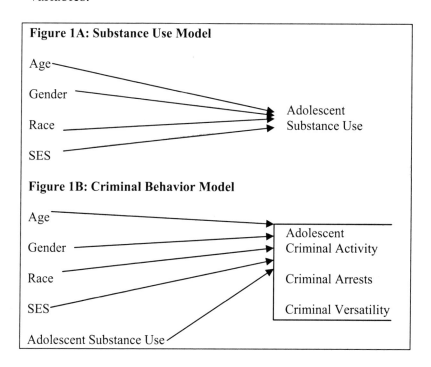

Figure 1A: Substance Use Model

Age
Gender
Race
SES

Adolescent Substance Use

Figure 1B: Criminal Behavior Model

Age
Gender
Race
SES
Adolescent Substance Use

Adolescent Criminal Activity
Criminal Arrests
Criminal Versatility

Question #1. Do adolescents cluster into several mutually exclusive groups of drug users with varying degrees of breadth and frequency of drug use?

Question #2. How do the adolescent drug use clusters associate with background characteristics, age, gender, race, and income subsidies?

Question #3. Are certain clusters of adolescent substance use more likely to be associated with self-report criminal activity, criminal arrests, and criminal versatility than other clusters?

Question #4. Do the adolescent drug use clusters support the life-course perspective and the gateway hypothesis found in the literature?

Question #5. How do patterns of adolescent drug use as assessed by clusters compare with those found using traditional measures of adolescent drug use?

Question #6. Is the pattern of relationships in Figure 1 similar when drug use is measured by clusters instead of traditional measures?

The six research questions will be analyzed using the 2001 NHSDA. The 2001 NHSDA is a multi-stage area probability sample of all non-institutionalized individuals over the age of 12 (Table 4) in the United States, including military personnel, those in group homes, shelters, and rooming houses (2001 NHSDA Codebook). The sub-sample consists of 17,429 adolescents.

Shortcomings and Contributions

The 2001 NHSDA data have several shortcomings. First, the data were based on self-reports of social environment, drug use, and crime characteristics, so it was difficult to verify the truthfulness on adolescents' responses. The NHSDA took precautions to reduce the amount of error in reporting by the adolescents. The adolescents were asked questions about their drug use and criminal behavior using headphones so the personal interviewer did not know the questions to which the adolescent was responding. Prior research stated adolescents over-report (Smart, et al., 1990), under-report (Grella, Chaiken, and Anglin, 1995), or report truthfully (Ellickson, et al., 1998) their substance use habits. For correlation research, this error tends to average out, and the findings are reliable (Carmines and Zeller, 1979). The data are cross-sectional, so temporal order is difficult to determine, but association still may be addressed. Finally, the data excluded all institutionalized individuals.

The present study contributes to the literature in four ways. First, few, if any, studies exist that use cluster analysis to examine adolescent drug use. This method will yield a better representation of adolescent drug use than measures presently found in the literature. It can distinguish among individuals who have similar but different drug use patterns that may be collapsed together in simpler drug use measures. Second, three types of criminal and deviant behavior will be presented. Few studies examine multiple measures of adolescent delinquency. In this case, both arrests and self-reported crime will be analyzed, as well as versatility for self-reported criminal offending. Third, because the 2001 NHSDA has over 17,000 adolescents, it allows robust estimates and examination of finer differences than smaller data sets. Whereas Hundleby and Mercer (1987) exclude measures of hard drug use because few adolescent use these drugs, cluster analysis can be used to examine these differences. Finally, a thorough comparison of 29 traditional drug use measures as they relate to both background variables and crime will be presented.

CHAPTER 4
Conducting a Study

SAMPLE

The 2001 National Household Survey on Drug Abuse (NHSDA) was a Multi-Stage Area Probability Sample of all non-institutionalized individuals over the age of 12 in the United States, including military personnel, those in group homes, shelters, and rooming houses (2001 NHSDA Codebook). The NHSDA conducted computer-assisted personal interviews of 68,929 individuals. The public use sample was 55,561 individuals because of "procedures to control the risk of disclosing the identity of any respondent" (2001 NHSDA Codebook, i-4).

The 2001 NHSDA targeted 3,600 individuals from each of the largest eight states and 900 from each of the other 42 states and the District of Columbia. Each of the larger states was divided into 48 sections, with a field interviewer responsible for each section. Each of the smaller states was divided into 12 sections. A computer chose a sample of addresses from each section, and the field interviewer screened the residents for eligibility at each sample address. A computer selected the final sample. The contact response rate was 92 percent, and the interview response rate was 73 percent. The survey sampled equal numbers of individuals in three age groups: 12 to 17 years, 18 to 25 years, and 26 years and older. The 12 to 17 years sub-sample of 17,429 adolescents will be used to assess adolescent substance use and crime. The mean age of the sub-sample was 14.5. Fifty percent were male, 20 percent lived in a household that received financial assistance, and 67 percent were non-Hispanic white (Table 1).

TABLE 1: Range, Mean, and Standard Deviation of Background Variables, Drug Variables, and Crime Variables

Variable	Range	Mean	S.D.
Age	12-17	14.474	1.680
Gender (M=1)	0-1	0.504	0.500
Inc. Subsidies*	0-1	0.203	0.402
Race (White)	0-1	0.667	0.471
Race (Black)	0-1	0.134	0.340
Race (Native)	0-1	0.016	0.124
Race (Asian)	0-1	0.032	0.175
Race (Multi)	0-1	0.019	0.137
Race (Hisp.)	0-1	0.133	0.340
Alcohol	0-365	12.992	38.856
Marijuana	0-365	12.733	51.537
Cocaine	0-365	0.584	9.342
Crack	0-365	0.180	5.758
Heroin	0-365	0.089	3.939
Inhalants	0-365	1.008	11.319
Pain Relievers	0-365	2.622	19.404
Hallucinogen	0-365	1.036	11.251
Tranquilizers	0-365	0.583	8.779
Stimulants	0-365	1.127	13.394
Sedatives	0-365	0.246	5.970
Meth.	0-365	0.352	7.431
SR Crime	0-1	0.315	0.464
SR Arrests	0-1	0.037	0.189
SR Versatility	0-6	0.534	0.988

n=17,429
*For income Subsidies, help=1, no help=0.

The 2001 NHSDA codebook did not yield specifics on how interviewers gained permission from parents to interview adolescents, nor did it give the refusal rates of parents or adolescents. The 2001 NHSDA was the 21st in a series of trend surveys aimed at measuring the prevalence and correlates of drug use within the United States (2001 NHSDA Codebook). The 2001 NHSDA had several strengths compared to other national surveys. It had a large sample of adolescents (n=17,429), which is the best way to generalize correlation and prevalence of drug use to the all adolescents within the United States (Dillman, 2000). The standard errors were small, and it was possible to examine phenomena with low incidence, such as hard drug use. Finally, it used multi-stage area-probability sample, an "equal probability of selection method" (EPSEM) that allowed the results to be generalized to the population. The NHSDA utilized personal interviews.

The 2001 NHSDA survey design had limitations as well. The data were self-reports, so it was difficult to verify the adolescents' truthfulness (2001 NHSDA codebook). Some researchers believed that adolescents under-report (Ellickson, et al., 1998) or over-report (Smart, et al., 1990) their substance use. Other research, however, found that adolescents reliably reported their drug use behavior (Smart, et al., 1990; Ellickson, et al., 1998), and those who did falsify substance use reports tended to under-report their use of substances (Grella, et al., 1995). Therefore, the 2001 NHSDA may have been a conservative estimate of adolescent substance use, so these findings were more likely to have Type II errors or false negatives (Kline, 1998). The 2001 NHSDA did take steps to eliminate this error, however, by having the adolescents use flash-cards and headsets to answer sensitive substance use questions, so the interviewer did not know to which question the adolescent was responding.

Because the data were cross-sectional, causal inferences about temporal order rest on interpretation, not evidence. The survey excluded institutionalized persons (slightly less than two percent of the population), including those in hospitals, prisons, nursing homes, and treatment centers. Therefore, the drug use and crime estimates from this analysis may be considered conservative because individuals in prisons and treatment centers may be more likely to use substances and commit crimes than those in the general population.

Substance Use Measurement

Adolescent substance use was assessed by instituting the cluster analysis method to create typologies of use. The illicit substances included in the analysis were: (1) alcohol, (2) marijuana, (3) cocaine, (4) crack, (5) heroin, (6) inhalants (such as paint thinner), (7) pain relievers (such as Oxycontin or codeine), (8) hallucinogens (such as Ecstasy, mushrooms, or lysergic acid), (9) tranquilizers (such as Valium), (10) sedatives (such as Quaaludes or barbiturates), (11) stimulants (such as amphetamines or Ritalin), and (12) methamphetamines. Technically, methamphetamines, cocaine, and crack are all stimulants, but in this analysis, these categories were mutually exclusive.

For each substance, the adolescents were asked "total number of days used [drug] in the past 12 months." The range for each of 12 drugs was zero to 365. On average, adolescents drank alcohol on 13 days over the past 12 months, smoked marijuana on 12 days, used pain relievers on three days, used inhalants, hallucinogens, and stimulants on one day, and used cocaine, crack, tranquilizers, heroin, sedatives, and methamphetamines less than one day.

Twenty-nine measures of adolescent substance use were abstracted from the literature. Because researchers used several individual measurements to operationalize drug use (Wechsler and Thum, 1973; Hundleby and Mercer, 1987; McGee, 1992; Donnermeyer, 1993; Benda, 1995; Havey and Dodd, 1995; Graham, 1996; Andrews, et al., 1997; Bahr, et al., 1998; Ellickson, et al., 1998; Diego, et al., 2003), dichotomized versions of all 12 drug use measures were created. If they used the drug, they were coded one; and if they did not, they were coded zero. In addition, ordinal-level measures of all 12 drugs were created using Donnermeyer's (1993) system of coding substance use. If the respondents had never used the drug, they were coded zero. If they had used the drugs once a month or less, they were coded one. If they used the drug between once a month and once a week, they were coded two. If they used the drug between once a week and two to three times a week, they were coded three. If they used the drug three or more times a week, they were coded four.

Five overall or sum measures of adolescents' substance use were also created: (1) an overall dichotomous measure, (2) an overall ordinal measure, (3) a summed measure of dichotomous use, (4) a summed measure of ordinal-level use, and (5) a Guttman Scale of substance use.

First, for the overall dichotomous measure of substance use (Novins and Mitchell, 1998; Keller, et al., 2002), if the adolescent had used any drug, they were coded one; if they did not, they were coded zero. Second, the overall ordinal-level measure was created using Donnermeyer's (1993) method (Akers and Cochran, 1985; Cochran and Akers, 1989; Smart, et al., 1990). Third, a summed measure of dichotomous use (Parker, et al., 1995), ranging from zero (no use on any drugs) to 12 (at least one use of each drug) was created. Fourth, for a summed measure of ordinal-level substance use (White, et al., 1985; Marcos, et al., 1986; Downs and Robertson, 1990; Stice, et al., 1993; Kinnier, et al., 1994; Duncan, et al., 1995; Stice and Barrera, 1995; Harrison, et al., 1997; Flannery, et al., 1999; Kelly, et al., 2002), the scale ranged from zero (no use on any drugs) to 48 (three or more times a week on all 12 drugs).

Finally, a Guttman scale of adolescent substance use (Brownfield and Sorenson, 1991; Chapple, et al., 2005) was analyzed using three measures of drug use: alcohol, marijuana, and hard drugs (combining the 10 measures of substance use in the NHSDA). Guttman scales assume a hierarchy of substance use by combining dichotomous measures where individuals at each step of the hierarchy are assumed to have met all the requirements of the previous steps (Jobling and Snell, 1961; Robinson, 1973). Adolescents who used only alcohol were coded one. Those who used marijuana, with the Guttman assumption that they had also used alcohol, were coded two. Adolescents who used at least one hard drug, with the Guttman assumption that they had used alcohol and marijuana as well, were coded three. Of course, this hierarchy did not exist in all cases, so a Guttman co-efficient of reproducibility statistic was used (Table 2), which is:

$$1 - \frac{\text{the total number of errors (1,304)}}{\text{the total number of guesses (52,287)}}$$

The Guttman co-efficient of reproducibility statistic was 0.975. A score above 0.80 is considered acceptable (Robinson, 1973).

TABLE 2: Guttman Scale Measure of Reproducibility			
	Alc Use	Mar Use	Hard Use	Number
	+	+	+	1,088
Scale Types	+	+	-	1,241
	+	-	-	3,106
	-	-	-	10,690
			Total=	16,125
	-	+	-	258
Mixed Types	+	-	+	458
	-	-	+	519
	-	-	+	69
			Total=	1,304
n=17,429				

Criminal Activity

Self-Report Criminal Activity. Six variables were used to construct the self-report criminal activity measure. The questions were, "During the past 12 months, how many times have you": (1) "gotten into a serious fight at school or work?" (2) "taken part in a fight where a group of your friends fought against another group?" (3) "carried a handgun?" (4) "sold illegal drugs?" (5) "stolen or tried to steal anything worth more than $50?" and (6) "attacked someone with the intent of seriously hurting them?" The answer categories for each question were: 0, 1-2 times, 3-5 times, 6-9 times, and 10 or more times. This measure was treated as a dichotomous variable rather than an additive scale because most of the variance existed between 0 and 1-

2 times. Respondents were coded one if they had committed any of these offenses, and zero if they had not committed any of them. Overall, 31.5 percent of the adolescents had committed at least one of the six offenses.

Self-Report Criminal Arrests. An overall measure of the seventeen criminal arrest variables was also created. The questions asked if "over the past 12 months," the adolescent had been "arrested and booked for" (1) motor vehicle theft, (2) larceny, (3) burglary or breaking and entering, (4) aggravated assault, (5) other assault, (6) robbery, (7) rape, (8) murder, homicide, or non-negligent manslaughter, (9) arson, (10) driving under the influence of alcohol or drugs, (11) drunkenness, (12) possession of tobacco, (13) possession or sale of drugs, (14) prostitution, (15) gender offense (excluding rape or prostitution), (16) fraud or stolen goods, and (17) other offenses not including minor traffic violations. Respondents were coded one if they had been arrested and booked for any of these offenses and zero if they had not committed any of them. Overall, 644 adolescents, or four percent of the sample, had been arrested and booked for at least one offense.

Criminal Versatility. Finally, A measure of criminal versatility was created using the same questions found in the self-report criminal activity measure but the dichotomous scores were summed to demonstrate versatility. Once again, adolescents received a score based on the number of different crimes they committed, not the frequency of committing individual crimes. The range was zero to six. The mean was 0.5 crimes.

A typology of criminal and deviant behavior was not created because the focus of this book was to introduce a typology of the drug user. The measures of drug use within the literature were far more misleading than those of criminal behavior. Creating a cluster analysis of adolescent crime is a project for a different book.

Background Variables

Age, gender, race, and family income subsidies were controlled in this study. Age was measured continuously with a range of 12 to 17 and a mean of 14.5. For gender, males were coded one and females coded zero, with 50 percent of the sample being boys. Family income subsidies was a dichotomous measure of whether the family received aid in the form of Social Security, Railroad Retirement, Supplemental Social Security payments, food stamps, public assistance, or welfare payments. Twenty percent of the adolescents in the sample had families who received government subsidies. Race and ethnicity was a series of dummy measures with values for Non-Hispanic whites (67%), African-Americans (13%), Asian-Americans (3%), Native Americans (2%), Latinos (13%), and individuals of multiple races (2%). For analysis, non-Hispanic whites were the omitted category.

Missing Data

The NHSDA used statistical imputation to estimate drug use by adolescents who were missing on any one of the 12 drugs. Specifically, the 2001 NHSDA used Predictive Mean Neighborhoods (PMN) to impute missing data (2001 NHSDA codebook). Also known as "hot decking," this method used cluster analysis to locate the "nearest neighbor" to each individual based on their use of other drugs, and it imputed that value. In other words, assuming that individual A had missing data on at least one drug, the individual B who was most similar on all other drugs to the individual A were set together. The missing data on A were imputed with B's responses (Little and Schnecker, 1995).

Of the 17,429 adolescents, 1,291 (7.5 percent) had substance use data imputed on one or more of the substance use variables. Two percent of the respondents had imputed data for alcohol use, which was the most of any single measure of the substance use variables. Imputed data for marijuana use, pain relief use, inhalant use, or hallucinogen use ranged from one to two percent. Less than one percent of the respondents had imputed data for cocaine use, crack use, heroin use, tranquilizer use, sedative use, stimulant use, and methamphetamine use.

A variable indicating imputed drug use was also created to examine the relationship between missing data in the substance use measures and the control variables age, race, gender, and family income subsidies. Respondents were coded one if they had imputed data on any of the 12 substances, and they were coded zero if they did not have imputed data on any of the 12 substances. Variables indicating imputed drug use on each of the 12 substances, respectively, was created as well. Using binary logistic regression, the overall drug use imputation variable was regressed on age, gender, income subsidies help, and race (Appendix A, Table 18). The results for gender and family income subsidies help were significant. Overall, males were 1.12 times more likely than females and individuals whose families received income subsidies were 1.25 times more likely than those whose families did not receive income subsidies to have data imputed on one or more of the drug use variables.

The dummy variable for imputed data was regressed on each individual substance use on age, gender (male), income subsidies help, and race, as well (please consult

Whiteford, 2004, Appendix D). Older adolescents were more likely than younger ones to have data imputed on marijuana use, cocaine use, and pain relief use. They were less likely than younger ones to have data imputed on sedative use and tranquilizer use. Males were more likely than females to have data imputed on sedatives. Hispanics were more likely than non-Hispanic whites to have data imputed on marijuana. Hispanics were less likely than non-Hispanic whites to have data imputed on stimulants. Asians were more likely than non-Hispanic whites to have data imputed on sedative use and tranquilizer use. African-Americans were less likely than non-Hispanic whites to have data imputed on hallucinogen use. Individuals whose families needed income subsidies were more likely to have alcohol use or inhalant use data imputed than those whose families did not need income subsidies.

What does drug imputation mean for this research? No discernable pattern developed for a specific group of adolescents across the 12 individual substances. Therefore, it is appropriate to use these data.

Finally, 46 adolescents had missing data on the self-report criminal activity and criminal versatility measures. Zeros were imputed for these individuals. The reasons for this imputation were twofold. First, 46 individuals out of 17,429 was only about one-third of one percent, which did not alter any tests of significance. Second, by imputing zero, the measures of association in correlation research were more conservative because it may reduce the strength of the relationship between substance use and other measures. Therefore, if anything, correlations between substance use were casualties of a type II error, or false negative (Kline, 1998).

Cluster Analysis

To examine alternative methods of measuring adolescent substance use, cluster analysis was used to create a typology of drug use. Cluster analysis categorizes individuals by systematically examining individual drug use patterns and forming groups out of individuals with closely matched drug use habits (Nunnally and Bernstein, 1994). It takes a heterogeneous sample (the 2001 NHSDA) and creates homogeneous groups based on the drug use variables (Muthen and Muthen, 2000). The cluster statistical method examined all 17,429 individuals based on the frequency of drug use over the past 12 months for alcohol, marijuana, crack, cocaine, heroin, methamphetamines, sedatives, stimulants, hallucinogens, inhalants, tranquilizers, and pain relievers. The two individuals who were most identical were grouped together, and then the individual who most closely matched the first two was grouped with them. If a sizeable difference occurs, then a new group forms (Nunnally and Bernstein, 1994). The difference was "the generalized Pythagorean distance between two points in Euclidean space" (Nunnally and Bernstein, 1994, 602). Euclidean distance is "intuitively appealing" because it "lends itself to powerful methods of analysis" (Nunnally and Bernstein, 1994, 603). Nunnally and Bernstein (1994) recommended use of Euclidean Distance in cluster analyses. Unfortunately, no statistical method exists to measure this sizeable difference, so visual inspection of the data was necessary to divide groups.

Individuals can be grouped using four methods. First, average-linkage measures the use patterns of the individuals in the group to link the next individual (Aldenderfer and Blashfield, 1984). For example, if one individual used alcohol 13 days a year, marijuana two days a year, and cocaine once a year, and the other individual in the group used alcohol fifteen days a year, marijuana two days a year, and never used cocaine, then the average linkage would average these individuals to alcohol 14 days, marijuana two days, and cocaine once every two years before adding a third member.

Second, complete-groups linkage, or furthest neighbor, uses the individual in the group who is most dissimilar to the rest of the individuals yet to be clustered (Aldenderfer and Blashfield, 1984). This method is biased toward finding more clusters with a smaller number of members than the other two methods (Aldenderfer and Blashfield, 1984).

Third, single-groups linkage, or nearest neighbor, uses the individual in the group who is most similar to the rest of the individuals yet to be clustered (Aldenderfer and Blashfield, 1984). This method is biased toward finding fewer clusters with more members than the other three methods (Aldenderfer and Blashfield, 1984).

The fourth type of linkage method is Ward's method. Ward's method minimizes within-group variance and maximizes between-group variance (Ward, 1963). This method tends to find clusters of relatively equally sizes (Aldenderfer and Blashfield, 1984).

This method was used in this study because it was important to separate individuals into groups with greater size especially if their use patterns appear to be similar. For example, if two individuals had similar use patterns for 11 of the 12 substances but were different on one (such as methamphetamine use where one individual uses it twice a year while the other uses it monthly or weekly), they should have been in a different groups, even if their frequency of use was identical on all of the other substances.

The Statistical Package for the Social Sciences (SPSS) was used to create the cluster groups. Of the 17,429 adolescents, 10,690 adolescents had not used any substance, so they were grouped together and omitted them from the rest of the cluster analysis. Under the "analyze" menu, the "classify" function was selected; followed by the "hierarchical cluster" option. "Squared Euclidean distance" and each of the clustering options: "average-linkage," "single-linkage," "complete-linkage," and Ward's method were used to analyze the remaining 6,739 adolescents who had used substances.

Cluster analysis has two advantages over measures of substance use found in the literature. First, it distinguishes among individuals who had different substance use patterns. Other methods, such as dichotomizing and then summing alcohol, marijuana, and hard drug use, put individuals with vastly different substance use patterns together if they have all at least tried the same drugs. Second, it creates groups, which are empirically closer to what actually happens in society. In other words, alternative methods tends to group members on arbitrary levels, either ordinal or nominal, based on their drug use, whereas cluster analysis grouped the individuals on how closely their use patterns match one another.

Cluster analysis has two primary disadvantages. As with most statistical practices, the data can be manipulated. In this case, this is most clearly choosing among Ward's method, average linkage, complete-groups linkage, and single-groups linkage. The four types of linkage presented different clustering results. Second, no statistical threshold exists for which clusters distinguish themselves. Therefore, visual inspection of the data is necessary to differentiate among groups of users.

Regression

Four types of regression methods were instituted to analyze the models in this study: multi-nomial logistic regression, binary logistic regression, ordered logit regression, and ordinary least squares regression. One of the four methods were employed for each model, contingent on how the dependent variable was measured and the assumptions of regression.

Multi-Nomial Logistic Regression on Substance Use. Multi-nomial logistic regression was used to investigate differences among the substance use groups by age, gender, race, and income subsidies. Multi-nomial logistic regression assumes that the dependent variable is nominal (SPSS, 2003). This analytic technique compares each of the nominal-level categories with the omitted group (Long, 1997). Multi-nomial logistic regression calculates each comparison within the omitted nominal variable at once. Therefore, the results are similar to a series of binary logistic regression runs, but the parameter estimates are based on the entire sample (Long, 1997). Because five cluster groups existed, a series of five multi-nomial logistic regressions were run so that each cluster group was omitted from one of the analyses. This allowed differences between each pair of clusters to be tested rather than compare each cluster to the abstainers.

Binary Logistic Regression. Binary logistic regression assumes that the dependent variable is dichotomous (Long, 1997; DeMaris, 1995). Binary logistic regression was used to explore the relationships between the drug use variables and the dichotomized measures of self-report criminal activity and criminal arrest. Binary logistic regression was also used to predict the dichotomous individual drug use measures and the overall dichotomous drug use measure found in the literature.

Both multi-nomial and binary logistic regression transforms the dependent variable into a latent variable where the odds that the event will occur are predicted (DeMaris, 1995). The odds ratio was interpreted at each level of the independent variable. In other words, if group 1 was regressed on age and had a significant odds ratio of 1.16, then for each year increase in age, individuals were 1.16 times more likely to be in group 1 than in the other groups combined.

An advantage to using both types of logistic regression is that the odds ratio of each cluster could be examined. A disadvantage to using these methods is that measurement error was not addressed (Long, 1997). Little error existed in the control variables, however, and because the dependent variables incorporated multiple constructs, the measurement error was more likely to average out than when using single-item indicators (Carmines and Zeller, 1979; Tabachnick and Fidell, 1996; Kline, 1998).

Ordered Logit Regression. Ordered logit regression was used for the ordinal drug use measures found in the literature. For ordinal-level measures, the assumption of linearity is particularly problematic. If age predicted the difference between categories zero and one (youths who have tried alcohol and those who have not), but did not explain the difference categories two and three (between regular and occasional drinkers), ordinary least squares analysis will lead to biased results (Fox, 1991). Ordered Logit Regression deals with skewed ordinal dependent variables and allows the researchers to test whether relationships are similar at each level of the dependent variable. For example, the ordinal-level drug use variables in this study had five levels of measurement. As long as the effects of the predictors were similar at each level of drug use, coefficients could be interpreted as valid for overall drug use. All correlations within the models were reported as parameter estimates, and they were interpreted similarly to coefficients in logistic regression.

Five link function options are available when using Ordered Logit Regression, which allowed for the best estimation of the model (SPSS, 2003). The five link functions have different assumptions surrounding their use. In this study, Logit and Cauchit seemed to be the most appropriate choices. After viewing the confusion matrix (comparing how well the link functions predict the categories within the tables), it was determined that Logit link function was the most suitable for this study.

The Pearson R-squared coefficient cannot be used when evaluating logistic regression or ordered logit regression. Therefore, the Nagelkerke R-squared was considered, which assumed values from zero to one and can be interpreted in a manner similar to the Pearson R squared (SPSS, 2003).

Ordinary Least Squares Regression. Finally, Ordinary least-squares regression was used for those models predicting criminal versatility. Several assumptions of regression had to be addressed for this analytic strategy to work with criminal versatility. The measure had to be a ratio-level variable, and it had to have a normal distribution, which it did after the responses were logged (base 10). The unstandardized coefficients were reported because they were intuitively more appealing. However, the Pearson R-squared was used to interpret the models' overall predictive values.

CHAPTER 5

Adolescent Substance Clusters

Six research questions will be explored throughout this book. First, do adolescents cluster into several mutually exclusive groups of drug users with varying degrees of breadth and frequency of drug use? Second, how do the adolescent drug use clusters associate with background characteristics, age, gender, race, and income subsidies? Third, are certain clusters of adolescent substance use more likely to be associated with self-report criminal activity, criminal arrests, and versatility than other clusters? Fourth, do the adolescent drug use clusters support the life-course perspective and the gateway hypothesis found in the literature? Fifth, how do patterns of adolescent drug use as assessed by clusters compare with those found using traditional measures of adolescent drug use? Finally, is the pattern of relationships in Figure 1 similar when drug use is measured by clusters instead of traditional measures? The first research question will be assessed in Chapter 5.

Cluster Analysis of Adolescent Substance Use
The 2001 NHSDA consisted of 17,429 adolescents. Four methods of cluster analysis were used to divide the adolescents into several mutually exclusive groups of substance users based on 12 types of illicit drugs: alcohol, marijuana, cocaine, crack, heroin, inhalants, pain relievers, hallucinogens, tranquilizers, stimulants, sedatives, and methamphetamines. Sixty-one percent (10,690) had not

experimented with substance use, so they grouped together. The remaining 6,739 adolescents were clustered by using the (1) average-linkage, (2) complete-linkage, (3) single-linkage, and (4) Ward's method of cluster analysis. Ward's method, which minimized within-group variance and maximized between-group variance (Ward, 1963), was the only method that distinguished classes of adolescents with large frequencies within each category and great variation between classes. Average-linkage, complete-linkage, and single-linkage, distinguished among classes of adolescent substance use, but the groups had low frequencies (less than 100) with little variation among the clusters.

Overall, five clusters emerged for evaluation (including the large group of non-users). The following figures demonstrate the five clusters using two different graphing techniques to amplify the differences among clusters. Table 3 and Figure 2 showed the clusters with the average

TABLE 3: Cluster Analysis (Raw Scores)

Drug	Abstainers	Dabblers	Benders	Deadeners	Heavies
Alcohol	0.00	14.68	153.91	50.19	100.93
Marijuana	0.00	7.55	23.06	158.97	300.97
Cocaine	0.00	0.20	1.07	14.87	8.74
Crack	0.00	0.01	0.24	5.56	2.64
Heroin	0.00	0.03	0.08	1.67	1.98
Inhalants	0.00	2.29	2.80	4.21	5.50
Pain Relievers	0.00	3.96	8.28	40.16	14.46
Hallucinogens	0.00	0.58	9.59	8.81	17.58
Tranquilizers	0.00	0.46	5.23	4.11	9.04
Stimulants	0.00	1.45	2.43	5.41	22.70
Sedatives	0.00	0.41	0.59	1.71	2.95
Meth.	0.00	0.24	0.68	1.21	10.76
n	10,690	5,470	545	351	373

daily use of each drug on the Y-axis and the types of drugs on the X-axis. Group one was called the "abstainers," none of whom used illicit substances. This group consisted of 10,690 adolescents. Group two was the called "dabblers" because they used substances occasionally. This group consisted of 5,470 adolescents. On average, this group

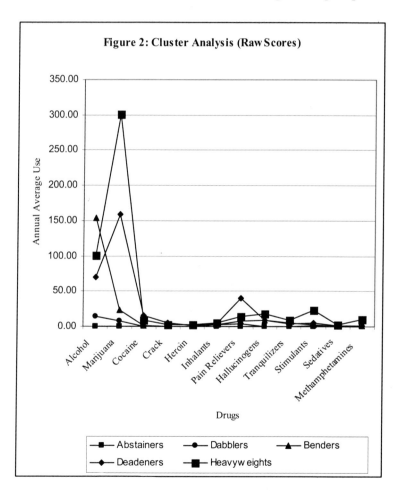

Figure 2: Cluster Analysis (Raw Scores)

used alcohol on 15 days over the past year. They used marijuana on eight days, pain relievers on four days, inhalants on two days, stimulants and hallucinogens on one day and cocaine, crack, heroin, tranquilizers, sedatives, and methamphetamines less than one time.

The final three groups could all be described as heavy users. They differed in the choice and frequency of substances used. Group three was called the "benders" because they drank alcohol frequently. This group consisted of 545 individuals. Over the past year, this group averaged 154 days of using alcohol, the most of any group. They used marijuana on 23 days, hallucinogens on 10 days, pain relievers on eight days, tranquilizers on five days, stimulants on two days, cocaine, sedatives, and methamphetamines on one day, and crack and heroin less than one time.

Group four was called the "deadeners" because they had the highest spike of use of any hard drug (pain relievers, such as Oxycontin, which deaden pain) across the three hard drug use groups. They also had elevated marijuana use. This group consisted of 351 adolescents. This cluster of adolescents used pain relievers, such as Oxycontin, on an average 40 days over the past year, a rate far above any of the other groups. They used marijuana on 159 days, alcohol on 70 days, cocaine on 15 days, hallucinogens on nine days, crack on six days, stimulants on five days, inhalants and tranquilizers on four days, sedatives and heroin on two days, and methamphetamines on one day.

The final group, group five, was called the "heavyweights" because this group averaged more substance use on eight of the 12 types of illicit drugs than any other cluster. This group consisted of 373 adolescents.

On average, this group used marijuana on 301 days, alcohol on 101 days, stimulants on 23 days, hallucinogens on 18 days, pain relievers on 14 days, methamphetamines on 11 days, tranquilizers and cocaine on nine days, inhalants on six days, sedatives and crack on three days, and heroin on two days.

Figure 2 was difficult to read because most substances have little to no use within each of the clusters. However, Table 4 and Figure 3 made the picture clearer. The z-scores of the substances were reported within each cluster in Table 4 and Figure 3.

TABLE 4: Cluster Analysis (Z-Scores)					
Drug	Abstainers	Dabblers	Benders	Deadeners	Heavyweights
Alcohol	-0.33	0.04	3.63	1.47	2.26
Marijuana	-0.25	-0.10	0.20	2.84	5.59
Cocaine	-0.06	-0.04	0.05	1.53	0.87
Crack	-0.03	-0.03	0.01	0.94	0.43
Heroin	-0.02	-0.01	-0.00	0.40	0.48
Inhalants	-0.09	0.11	0.16	0.28	0.40
Pain Relievers	-0.14	0.07	0.29	1.94	0.61
Hallucinogens	-0.09	-0.04	0.76	0.69	1.47
Tranquilizers	-0.07	-0.01	0.53	0.40	0.96
Stimulants	-0.08	0.02	0.10	0.32	1.16
Sedatives	-0.04	0.03	0.06	0.25	0.45
Meth.	-0.05	-0.02	0.04	0.12	1.40
n	10,690	5,470	545	351	373

The z-scores were on the Y-axis and the substances were on the X-axis of the graph. The lines of abstainers and dabblers remained close together and virtually parallel. The benders, deadeners, and heavyweights, however, were more easily distinguished from each other using the z-score method. Using this graph, the heavyweights seemed to pull away from the benders and deadeners, and the deadeners distinguished themselves from the benders, as well. All three heavy use groups have substances that stand apart (greater than 1.9 standard deviations above the mean) from the others based on z-scores. For the benders, alcohol was 3.63 standard deviations above the mean.

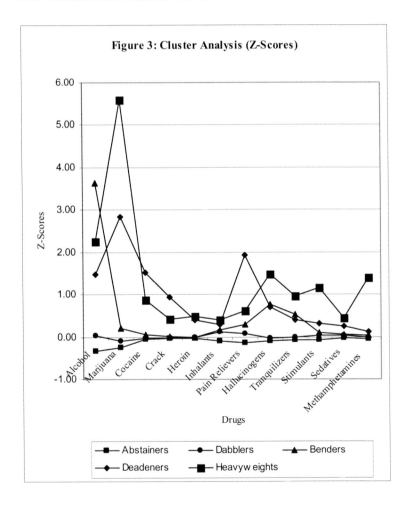

Figure 3: Cluster Analysis (Z-Scores)

For the deadeners, marijuana was 2.84 and pain relievers 1.94 standard deviations above the mean. For the heavyweights, marijuana was 5.59 and alcohol was 2.26 standard deviations above the mean.

Table 5 presented the ranges, means, and standard deviations of the clusters reported as dummy variables. Overall, 61 percent of the adolescents were abstainers. Thirty-one percent were dabblers. Three percent were benders. Two percent were deadeners and heavyweights, respectively. Excluding the abstainers, each cluster had at least one individual who used each of the 12 substances. Therefore, it was not breadth of use which distinguished the clusters from each other but the depth of use on particular substances that best classified the adolescents.

TABLE 5: Range, Mean, and Standard Deviation of Cluster Groups			
Variable	Range	Mean	S.D.
Cluster: Abstainers	0-1	0.613	0.487
Cluster: Dabblers	0-1	0.314	0.464
Cluster: Benders	0-1	0.031	0.174
Cluster: Deadeners	0-1	0.020	0.140
Cluster: Heavyweights	0-1	0.021	0.145
n=17,429			

Bivariate Analysis of Adolescent Drug Use Clusters
The distribution of clusters were presented by age, gender, income subsidies, and race in a cross-tabulation to understand the clusters more clearly (Table 6).

Abstainers. Sixty-one percent of adolescents clustered as abstainers. The likelihood of being an abstainer declined steadily with age. Being an abstainer was unrelated to gender or income, but it was related to race/ethnicity, with

Asian-Americans (72%) being most likely to abstain, followed by African-Americans (69%), Hispanics (63%), adolescents of multiple race (60%), non-Hispanic whites (59%), and Native Americans (56%).

Dabblers. Thirty-one percent of adolescents clustered as dabblers. The likelihood of being a dabbler increased steadily by age. Females were somewhat more likely to be dabblers than were males. Being a dabbler was unrelated to income subsidies, but it was related to race/ethnicity, with non-Hispanic whites (33%) being most likely to be dabblers, followed by Native Americans (32%), adolescents of multiple race (31%), Hispanics (30%), African-Americans (26%), and Asian-Americans (25%).

Benders. Three percent of adolescents clustered as benders. Once again, the likelihood of being a bender increased steadily by age. Benders were unrelated to gender or income subsidies, but they were related to race/ethnicity. Non-Hispanic whites (3%) and Native Americans (3%) were most likely to be benders, followed by adolescents of multiple race (2%), Hispanics (2%), African-Americans (2%), and Asian-Americans (2%).

Deadeners. Two percent of adolescents clustered as deadeners. The likelihood of being a deadener also increased steadily by age. Being a deadener was unrelated to gender (male) or income subsidies, but it was related to race/ethnicity, with Native Americans (6%) being most likely to be deadeners, followed by Hispanics (3%), non-Hispanic whites (2%), adolescents of multiple race (2%), African-Americans (2%), and Asian-Americans (<1%).

Heavyweights. Two percent of adolescents clustered as heavyweights. The likelihood of being a heavyweight increased steadily by age. Those who received income

TABLE 6: Descriptive Statistics					
n=17,429	Abs	Dab	Ben	Dead	Heavies Total
Age 12	2467	298	12	6	3	2786
Percentage	88.5	10.7	0.4	0.2	0.1	99.9
Age 13	2415	587	21	12	12	3047
Percentage	79.3	19.3	0.7	0.4	0.4	100.1
Age 14	1999	922	51	42	28	3042
Percentage	65.7	30.3	1.7	1.4	0.9	100.0
Age 15	1514	1141	114	69	73	2911
Percentage	52.0	39.2	3.9	2.3	2.5	99.9
Age 16	1286	1267	147	127	125	2952
Percentage	43.6	42.9	5.0	4.3	4.2	100.0
Age 17	1009	1255	200	95	132	2691
Percentage	37.5	46.6	7.4	3.5	4.9	99.9
Female	5204	2864	269	159	139	8635
Percentage	60.3	33.2	3.1	1.8	1.6	100.0
Male	5486	2606	276	192	234	8794
Percentage	62.4	29.6	3.1	2.2	2.7	100.0
Inc Help (n)	8532	4380	426	265	282	13885
Percentage	61.4	31.5	3.1	1.9	2.0	99.9
Inc Help (y)	2158	1090	119	86	91	3544
Percentage	60.9	30.8	3.4	2.4	2.6	100.1
White	6885	3857	398	228	258	11626
Percentage	59.2	33.2	3.4	2.0	2.2	100.0
Afr-Amer	1607	593	52	40	37	2329
Percentage	69.0	25.5	2.2	1.7	1.6	100.0
Native Amer	152	87	7	15	13	274
Percentage	55.5	31.8	2.6	5.5	4.7	100.1
Multiple Race	200	102	9	8	13	332
Percentage	60.2	30.7	2.7	2.4	3.9	99.9
Hispanic	1451	696	67	57	48	2319
Percentage	62.6	30.0	2.9	2.5	2.1	100.1
Asian-Amer	395	135	12	3	4	549
Percentage	71.9	24.6	2.2	0.5	0.7	99.9
Total	10690	5470	545	351	373	17429
Percentage	61.3	31.4	3.1	2.0	2.1	99.9

subsidies were slightly more likely to be heavyweights than those adolescents who did not receive income subsidies. Being a heavyweight was unrelated to gender (male), but it was related to race/ethnicity, with Native Americans (6%) being most likely to be heavyweights, followed by Hispanics (3%), non-Hispanic whites (2%), adolescents of multiple race (2%), African-Americans (2%), and Asian-Americans (<1%).

Overall, age and percent within cluster varied positively for all of the groups, with the result that the residual category—abstainers—became smaller in each older age group. A greater percentage of males than females were present in every cluster except for dabblers. In all five clusters, those who received income subsidies and those who did not receive income subsidies were nearly identical (within one percent). Asian-Americans had their highest percent in abstainers. Non-Hispanic whites had their highest percentage in the dabblers and benders. Native-Americans had their highest percentage in the deadeners and heavyweights. African-Americans and Asian-Americans had a smaller percentage than non-Hispanic whites in all four of the drug use clusters.

The fourth research question states, "do the adolescent drug use clusters support the Life-Course Perspective and the Gateway Hypothesis found in the literature?" One would expect to find fewer abstainers at older than at younger ages, and a reverse pattern for the substance use groups, especially for the benders, deadeners, and heavyweights. These data supported the gateway hypothesis. In all four drug using clusters, there were a greater number of older substance users than younger substance users across the age categories (Figure 4). Based on percentage, over 60 percent of the benders, deadeners, and heavyweights were in the two oldest age categories, 16 and 17. This was the opposite for the abstainers, where younger abstainers outnumbered older ones, where over 60 percent of the abstainers were in the three youngest age categories, 12, 13, and 14. The results were presented in

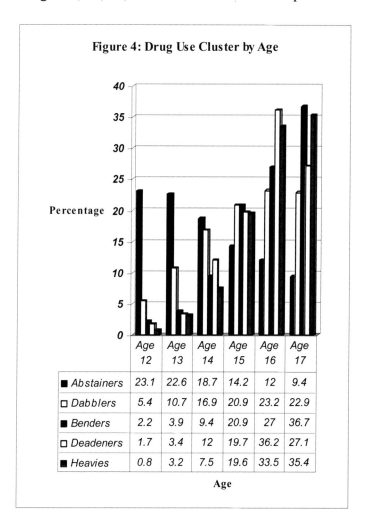

Figure 4: Drug Use Cluster by Age

	Age 12	Age 13	Age 14	Age 15	Age 16	Age 17
■ Abstainers	23.1	22.6	18.7	14.2	12	9.4
□ Dabblers	5.4	10.7	16.9	20.9	23.2	22.9
■ Benders	2.2	3.9	9.4	20.9	27	36.7
□ Deadeners	1.7	3.4	12	19.7	36.2	27.1
■ Heavies	0.8	3.2	7.5	19.6	33.5	35.4

Age

Figure 4 using a bar chart rather than a line graph because these data were cross-sectional, so causal inferences could not be determined. This chart demonstrated, however, that the heavy drug use groups were larger for every year older. Therefore, adolescents may indeed graduate from abstainers, through dabblers, and for some, to benders, deadeners, or heavyweights. The life-course perspective will be discussed in Chapter 7.

CHAPTER 6

Examining the Substance Clusters

Multi-Variate Analysis of Adolescent Drug Use Clusters
To gain a greater insight into the clusters, the five adolescent drug use groups were regressed on the background variables (age, gender, income subsidies help, and race) (Tables 19 though 23, Appendix B). Together, the five drug use clusters formed a single nominal measure of adolescent substance use. Multi-nomial logistic regression was the most appropriate multi-variate statistical method to analyze these clusters. Basically, each cluster is compared against an omitted cluster in each step of the multi-nomial logistic regression while holding the other clusters constant. In other words, in Table 19, the omitted category was the abstainers, and column one of Table 19, compared the dabblers against the abstainers while holding the benders, deadeners, and heavyweights constant. Therefore, the second research question is addressed in this chapter: "How do the adolescent drug use clusters associate with background characteristics, age, gender, race, and income subsidies?"

The results varied depending on which cluster was omitted. Therefore, five different multi-nomial logistic regressions were presented, with each cluster omitted once throughout the set. Overall, 20 combinations existed, but each individual combination between clusters was presented twice. For example, in column one of Table 19, abstainers were omitted and compared to dabblers, and in column one of Table 20, dabblers were omitted and compared to abstainers. Basically, the columns were inverses of each other. Each comparison is discussed only the first time it emerged.

The dabblers were compared against the abstainers while holding the benders, deadeners, and heavyweights constant in column one of Table 19 (and column one of Table 20). Age, gender (male), and three racial/ethnic groups were significant predictors of being a dabbler (Table 19). For every year older, adolescents were 1.58 (b=0.457) times more likely to be dabblers than abstainers. Males were 15 percent (b=-0.161) less likely than females to be dabblers than abstainers. African-Americans were 38 percent (b=-0.477), Asian-Americans were 49 percent (b=-0.675), and Hispanics were 16 percent (b=-0.171) less likely than non-Hispanic whites to be dabblers than abstainers. For the entire analysis (all of the columns), the pseudo R-squared (Nagelkerke) was 0.184, so 18 percent of the variance in the drug clusters was accounted for by age, race, gender, and income subsidies.

Next, the benders were compared against the abstainers while holding the dabblers, deadeners, and heavyweights constant in column two of Table 19 (column one of Table 21). Age and three racial/ethnic groups were significant predictors of being a bender (Table 19). For every year older, adolescents were 2.13 (b=0.756) times more likely to be benders than abstainers. African-Americans were 51 percent (b=0.701), Asian-Americans were 60 percent (b=0.927), and Hispanics were 24 percent (b=0.271) less likely than non-Hispanic whites to be benders than abstainers.

The deadeners were compared against the abstainers while holding the dabblers, benders, and heavyweights constant in column three of Table 19 (column one of Table 22). Again, age and three racial/ethnic groups were significant predictors of being a deadener (Table 19). For every year older, adolescents were 2.01 (b=0.669) times more likely to be deadeners than abstainers. African-Americans were 34 percent (b=0.414) and Asian-Americans were 83 percent (b=1.749) less likely than non-Hispanic whites to be deadeners than abstainers, whereas Native Americans were 2.70 (b=0.996) times more likely than non-Hispanic whites to be deadeners than abstainers.

The heavyweights were compared against the abstainers in column four of Table 19 (column one of Table 23). On age and race/ethnicity, the picture was almost identical for heavyweights as it was for benders and deadeners. The exception was gender. Heavyweights was the only cluster to which males were significantly more likely then females to belong. For every year older, adolescents were 2.28 (b=0.824) times more likely to be heavyweights than abstainers. Males were 1.58 (b=0.460) more likely than females to be heavyweights than abstainers. African-Americans were 47 percent (b=0.638) times and Asian-Americans were 80 percent (b=1.629) less likely than non-Hispanic whites to be heavyweights than abstainers, whereas Native Americans were 2.04 (b=0.710) times more likely than non-Hispanic whites to be heavyweights than abstainers.

Overall, older adolescents were more likely to be users than abstainers, and this relationship became more substantial in the heavy use groups (benders, deadeners, and heavyweights). Across all abstainer relationships, Asian-Americans and African-Americans were significantly less likely than whites to use substances. Males were significantly more likely than females to be heavyweights than abstainers, but females were more likely than males to be dabblers than abstainers. This demonstrated a U-shaped curve, in which males were more likely than females to be both abstainers and heavyweights.

Table 19 presented the relationships between the abstainers and the substance use groups. It is important to understand whether clusters of users differ from one another as well as from non-users. Therefore, a multi-nomial logistic regression was run four more times, with each of the user groups as the omitted category throughout each run, respectively.

The dabbler cluster and its relationships to the other drug clusters were examined in Table 20. The benders were compared with the dabblers in column two of Table 20 (column two of Table 21). Only age was a significant predictor of being a bender rather than a dabbler (Table 20). For every year older, adolescents were 1.35 (b=0.299) times more likely to be benders than dabblers.

The deadeners were compared against the dabblers in column three of Table 20 (column two of Table 22). Age, gender (males), and Native Americans were significant predictors of being a deadener (Table 20). For every year older, adolescents were 1.27 (b=0.242) times more likely to be deadeners than dabblers. Males were 1.33 (b=0.287) times more likely than females to be deadeners than dabblers. Native Americans were 2.74 (b=1.008) times more likely than non-Hispanic whites to be deadeners than dabblers.

The heavyweights were compared against the dabblers in column four of Table 20 (column two of Table 23). Age, gender (male), and two racial/ethnic groups were significant predictors of being a heavyweight (Table 20). For every year older, adolescents were 1.44 (b=0.367) times more likely to be heavyweights than dabblers. Males were 1.86 (b=0.621) times more likely than females to be heavyweights than dabblers. Native Americans were 2.06 (b=0.723) times and adolescents of multiple races were 1.93 (b=0.658) times more likely than non-Hispanic whites to be heavyweights than dabblers.

Overall, older adolescents were more likely to be in a heavy use group (benders, deadeners, or heavyweights) than dabblers. Once again, gender (male) had the U-shaped relationship with dabblers. Males were more likely than females to be abstainers, but they were also more likely to be hard users.

Finally, the relationships among the hard use groups were explored to examine differences among the small population of adolescents who use substances habitually in Tables 21 through 23. The deadeners were compared against the benders in column three of Table 21 (column three of Table 22). Native Americans were (3.69 [b=1.307] times) significantly more likely than non-Hispanic whites to be deadeners than benders.

The heavyweights were compared against the benders in column four of Table 21 (column three of Table 23). Gender (male) and Native American stauts were significant predictors of being a heavyweight (Table 8). Males were 1.66 (b=0.504) times more likely than females to be heavyweights than benders. Native Americans were 2.78 (b=1.021) times more likely than non-Hispanic whites to be heavyweights than benders.

Lastly, the heavyweights were compared against the deadeners in column four of Table 22 (column four of Table 23). Age and gender (male) were significant predictors of being a heavyweight (Table 22). For every year older, adolescents were 1.13 (b=0.125) times more likely to be heavyweights than deadeners. Males were 1.40 (b=0.334) times more likely than females to be heavyweights than benders.

Substantial differences were few among the hard use groups. The significant differences existed mostly between the heavyweights and the other two hard use groups. Older adolescents were more likely than younger ones to be heavyweights than deadeners. Males were more likely than females to be heavyweights than either benders or deadeners, and Native Americans were more likely than whites to be deadeners or heavyweights than benders.

Summary and Conclusion
Using Ward's method, adolescents clustered into five types of substance users. Adolescents with no substance use experience were abstainers. Adolescents with minimal substance use experience across many drugs were dabblers. Adolescents who drank frequently with elevated casual drug use (compared to dabblers) were benders. Adolescents who used marijuana and pain relievers, with elevated casual drug use (compared to dabblers) were deadeners. Adolescents who used drugs frequently and smoked marijuana almost daily were heavyweights.

At the bi-variate level, age appeared to be the most intriguing variable. For every year older, abstainers lost group members, whereas dabblers, benders, deadeners, and heavyweights all increased in size.

The multi-variate columns provided some insight into these relationships. In general, for every year older, adolescents were significantly more likely to be in harder drug use groups. For example, abstainers to dabblers or deadeners to heavyweights. This finding was consistent with the literature, which found that older adolescents were more likely than younger adolescents to use drugs (White, et al., 1985; Cochran, 1993; Benda, 1995; Duncan, et al., 1995; Stice and Barrera, 1995; Wood, et al., 1995; Andrews, et al., 1997; Akers and Lee, 1998; Bahr, et al., 1998; Parker, et al., 2000; Goode, 2001; Keller, et al., 2002).

Males were less likely than females to be dabblers, but males were more likely than females to be abstainers, deadeners, or heavyweights. In other words, females were more often casual users than males, but males were more likely to be heavy users than females. This was inconsistent with literature. Duncan and associates (1995) found girls started using substances at younger ages than boys, but boys were more likely to increase use faster than girls. However, Simons-Morton and Chen (2006) found that boys started using substance at younger ages than girls, but girls were more likely to increase use faster than boys. Boys were more likely than girls to be heavy users (Wilsnack and Wilsnack, 1980; Cochran, 1993; Duncan, et al., 1995; Osgood, et al., 1996; Bensley, et al., 1999; Parker, et al., 2000)

Very little difference existed between those whose families received subsidies and those whose families did not as it related to the type of user. This finding was consistent with previous research that found no differences among classes and their use of substances (Arafat, 1979; Hundleby and Mercer, 1987; McGee, 1992; Benda, 1995; Parker, et al., 1995).

In general, non-Hispanic whites were more likely than African-Americans or Asian-Americans to be in harder drug use groups, but less likely than Native Americans to be in harder drug use groups. This was consistent with prior work, which found that non-Hispanic whites were significantly more likely than adolescents of other races to use substances (Benda, 1995; Parker, et al., 1995; Wood, et al., 1995; Graham, et al., 1996), and prior work that reported Native Americans were significantly more likely than non-Hispanic whites to use substances (Wood, et al., 1995; Novins and Mitchell, 1998).

In conclusion, although the drug clusters adhere to standard analytic techniques requirements, the results were similar to correlations found in the literature between age, income subsidies, and race and adolescent substance use. The relationship between gender and substance use patterns was substantively different using cluster analysis than standard analytical techniques. Boys were more likely than girls to be a hard user or an abstainer, and girls were more likely than boys to be dabblers. No previous research that explored this unique U-shaped relationship between males' and females' drug use patterns. The drug use clusters demonstrated the new and interesting correlation with gender, and they may also be able to disentangle the drug use-crime relationship.

CHAPTER 7

Adolescent Substance Use and Crime

Prior work has established that the relationship between adolescent substance use and criminal and deviant behavior is significant and substantial. The relationship among the five drug use clusters and three measures of criminal and deviant behavior: self-report criminal activity, self-report criminal arrests, and versatility in criminal activity will be explored in this chapter.

All three measures of criminal and deviant behavior were included to increase the reliability of this study and to examine both activity and versatility. Thirty-two percent of adolescents committed some type of criminal behavior (Table 1). Four percent of adolescents reported being arrested and booked for criminal activity. Of the six measures of self-report crime and deviance, adolescents reported committing an average of less than one type of crime per year (0.534). The third and fourth research questions will be addressed in this chapter: "Are certain clusters of adolescent substance use more likely to be associated with self-report criminal activity, criminal arrests, and versatility than other clusters?" and "Do the adolescent drug use clusters support the Life-Course Perspective and the Gateway Hypothesis found in the literature?"

Multi-Variate Analysis of Adolescent Drug Use Clusters
To examine the third research question, the three measures
of criminal activity were regressed on the drug use clusters
and background variables. Self-report criminal activity and
self-report criminal arrests were both dichotomous
variables, so a series of binary logistic regressions were run
to analyze their relationships with adolescent substance use.
Versatility of criminal behavior, however, was an interval
variable, so a series of ordinary least squares regressions
were run to analyze it.

Self-Report Criminal Activity
The 2001 NHSDA asked adolescents several questions
about their criminal activity. If they had committed any of
the crimes, regardless of severity, they were coded one; if
they did not, then they were coded zero. The mean for
criminal activity was 0.315, so about 32 percent of the
adolescents had committed a crime (Table 1).

To analyze self-report criminal activity, a series of five
binary logistic regressions were run with self-report
criminal activity as the dependent variable and the
background variables (age, gender [male], race, and income
subsidies) and the drug use clusters as the independent
variables. One cluster was omitted in each of the
regressions to analyze the differences among the types of
clusters.

The fourth research question was "Do adolescent drug
use clusters support the life-course perspective and the
gateway hypothesis found in the literature?" To answer
this question, a series of five more binary logistic
regressions were run to analyze the interaction between age
and cluster on self-report criminal activity. The results
were presented in five tables with two sets in each table

(one with the regular column and one with the interaction column).

In set one of Tables 24 through 28 (Appendix C), the coefficients for the background variables were exactly the same. Coefficients for drug clusters varied, however, because of the change in the omitted cluster. Age, gender (male), income subsidies, and race were all significantly correlated with self-report criminal activity. For every year older, adolescents were 11 percent (b=-0.116) less likely to report criminal behavior. Males were 1.55 (b=0.433) times more likely than females to report committing criminal activity. Those who received income subsidies were 1.33 (b=0.284) times more likely than those who did not receive income subsidies to report criminal activity. African-Americans were 1.68 (b=0.515) times, Native Americans were 1.40 (b=0.334) times, adolescents of multiple races were 1.39 (b=0.333) times, and Hispanics were 1.28 (b=0.246) times more likely than non-Hispanic whites to report committing criminal behavior.

Table 24 showed the most straightforward comparison, where each type of user was contrasted with abstainers. Dabblers were 2.57 (b=0.945) times, benders were 6.05 times (b=1.799) times, deadeners were 8.41 (b=2.129) times, and heavyweights were 11.12 (b=2.409) times more likely than abstainers to report committing a criminal act over the past year. Thus, dabblers, benders, deadeners, and heavyweights were significantly more likely than abstainers to report committing crime (Table 24). In Table 25, dabblers were the omitted category. Benders were 2.351 times (b=0.855) times, deadeners were 3.27 (b=1.184) times, and heavyweights were 4.32 (b=1.464) times more likely than dabblers to report committing a criminal act over the past year. Thus, benders, deadeners, and heavyweights were significantly more likely than dabblers to report committing crime (Table 25). In Table 26, benders were the omitted category. Deadeners were 1.39 (b=0.330) times and heavyweights were 1.84 (b=0.609) times more likely than benders to report committing a criminal act over the past year. Thus, deadeners and heavyweights were significantly more likely than benders to report committing crime (Table 26).

Finally, in Table 27, deadeners were the omitted category. The relationship between deadeners and heavyweights in self-report criminal behavior did not reach significance. To analyze this relationship further, the deadeners and heavyweights were abstracted from the data set and a dichotomous variable was created with heavyweights coded one and deadeners coded zero. A binary logistic regression of self-report crime was regressed on the background variables and the dichotomous heavyweight-deadener variable (Whiteford, 2004, Appendix E). This regression consisted of 724 adolescents. The deadener-heavyweight relationship was marginally significant (b=0.289, p<0.080), with heavyweights being 1.34 times more likely than deadeners to commit crime.

For the multi-nomial logistic regression reported in Tables 24 through 28, the pseudo R-squared (Nagelkerke) was 0.121, so 12 percent of the variance in self-report criminal activity was accounted for by age, race, gender (male), income subsidies, and drug use.

Self-Report Criminal Behavior and the Life-Course Perspective
The fourth research question addresses whether evidence from adolescent drug use clusters supported the life-course perspective and the gateway hypothesis found in the

literature. If this hypothesis is true, one expects to find a stronger relationship between drug use groups and crime among younger than older substance users. To test the hypothesis, multiplicative terms were created for age and each cluster. In sets two of Tables 24 through 38 (including the criminal arrests and versatility), interactions between age and the five drug use cluster groups on crime were included. The four interactions in Figures 5 through 7 were assessed using bar charts rather than line graphs because these data were cross-sectional, so causal inferences among the data were difficult to determine. The model Chi-squares between set one and set two of Tables 24 through 28 changed significantly, so the results of the interactions can be interpreted.

The life-course perspective, which states that life-course-persistent delinquents begin their offending (and using substances) earlier, and commit more crimes (and used more substances), than adolescent-limited youths (Moffitt, 1993; Moffitt, 1997), so older substance use groups probably contain a mix of adolescent-limited and life-course-persistent youths, whereas younger substance users are most likely to be life-course-persistent youths.

Overall, older adolescents were less likely than younger ones to report committing crimes (Figure 5). The individuals who dabble at early ages were moderately criminal, but those who dabble at 17 were not much different than abstainers. At age 12 the benders had the highest rates of crime, but at age 17 the benders were significantly less likely than the deadeners or heavyweights to commit crime. This finding might not be reliable because only 12 benders were 12 years old. Therefore, becoming a dabbler or bender earlier in their adolescent years had a greater impact on whether or not they commit crime than becoming a dabbler or bender later in adolescence.

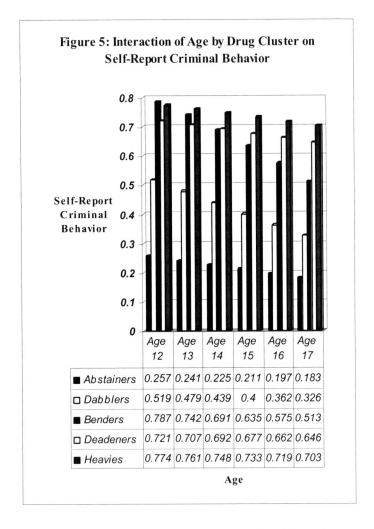

Figure 5: Interaction of Age by Drug Cluster on Self-Report Criminal Behavior

	Age 12	Age 13	Age 14	Age 15	Age 16	Age 17
■ Abstainers	0.257	0.241	0.225	0.211	0.197	0.183
□ Dabblers	0.519	0.479	0.439	0.4	0.362	0.326
■ Benders	0.787	0.742	0.691	0.635	0.575	0.513
□ Deadeners	0.721	0.707	0.692	0.677	0.662	0.646
■ Heavies	0.774	0.761	0.748	0.733	0.719	0.703

Age

The 2001 NHSDA was cross-sectional, but these results supported the life-course perspective. Adolescents who were in one of the four drug-using categories were more likely to commit crimes than adolescents who were abstainers. The differences between the dabblers and benders and the abstainers decreased by age. This was inconsistent with the explanation that adolescent-limited youths were dabblers and benders in late teen years (Table 6), so their rate of crime was closer to that of abstainers. Being a dabbler or bender at an early age, however, had a greater impact on criminal offending than being an abstainer. In fact, benders at age 12 (n=12) had the greatest percentage of criminal offenders compared to any other group, but by age 17, benders (n=200) were significantly less likely than deadeners or heavyweights to commit crime. These results must be viewed with some caution, however, because relatively few younger adolescents were hard drug users.

Self-Report Criminal Arrests
An alternative measure of crime in the 2001 NHSDA was arrests. If adolescents reported being arrested for any crimes, they were coded one; if they were not, then they were coded zero. The mean for criminal arrests was 0.037, so about four percent of adolescents had been arrested for a crime. Identical to self-report criminal activity, a series of five binary logistic regressions were run with self-report criminal arrests as the dependent variable and the background variables (age, gender [male], race, and income subsidies) and the drug use clusters as the independent variables in Tables 29 through 33 (Appendix D).

Once again, the coefficients for the background variables were exactly the same in Tables 29 through 33. Age, gender (male), income subsidies, and race were all significantly correlated with self-report criminal arrests.

For every year older, adolescents were 1.17 (b=0.160) times more likely to report criminal arrests. Whereas adolescent age and self-report criminal activity were negatively correlated (Tables 29 through 33), age and self-report criminal arrests were positively correlated. Males were 1.99 (b=0.689) times more likely than females to report arrests. Those who received income subsidies were 1.51 (b=0.412) times more likely than those who did not receive income subsidies to report arrests. African-Americans were 1.64 (b=0.493) times, Native Americans were 1.80 (b=0.589) times, adolescents of multiple races were 1.79 (b=0.582) times, and Hispanics were 1.48 (b=0.394) times more likely than non-Hispanic whites to report criminal arrests.

In Table 29, abstainers were the omitted category. Dabblers were 4.10 (b=1.410) times, benders were 10.08 times (b=2.311) times, deadeners were 14.79 (b=2.694) times, and heavyweights were 20.64 (b=3.027) times more likely than abstainers to report being arrested over the past year. Thus, dabblers, benders, deadeners, and heavyweights were significantly more likely than abstainers to report criminal arrests (Table 29). In Table 30, dabblers were the omitted category. Benders were 2.46 times (b=0.901) times, deadeners were 3.61 (b=1.284) times, and heavyweights were 5.03 (b=1.617) times more likely than dabblers to report being arrested over the past year. Thus, benders, deadeners, and heavyweights were significantly more likely than dabblers to report criminal arrests (Table 30). In Table 31, benders were the omitted category. Deadeners were 1.47 (b=0.383) times and heavyweights were 2.05 (b=0.716) times more likely than benders to report being arrested over the past year. Thus, deadeners and heavyweights were significantly more likely than benders to report criminal arrests (Table 31).

Finally, in Table 32, deadeners were the omitted category. Once again, the relationship between the deadeners and heavyweights did not reach significance. Using the same technique that was instituted in the previous section, a binary logistic regression of criminal arrests on the heavyweight-deadener dichotomized variable was run and held the background variables constant (Whiteford, 2004, Appendix E). Once again, the relationship was marginally significant (b=0.327, p<0.077) in this subset of 724 adolescents. Therefore, heavyweights were 1.39 times more likely than deadeners to be arrested. For the multi-nomial logistic regression, the pseudo R-squared (Nagelkerke) is 0.177, so 18 percent of the variance in self-report criminal arrests was accounted for by age, race, gender (male), income subsidies, and drug use.

Criminal Arrests and the Life-Course Perspective

Once again, this paper examined whether the effect of drug clusters depended on age. In sets two of Tables 29 through 33, the four interactions between age and the five drug use cluster groups were included (omitting one in each table). The model Chi-squares between set one and set two of Tables 29 through 33 did not change significantly, so interpretations of the interactions were speculative.

Although older adolescents were more likely to report having been arrested for criminal behavior, this phenomenon was amplified for deadeners and heavyweights when compared to benders (Table 31 and Figure 6). At age 12, the likelihood that a deadener would be arrested was less than that of a bender and similar to that of a dabbler; by the age of 17, however the likelihood a deadener would be arrested was the same as a heavyweight. Becoming (or staying) a deadener or heavyweight later in their adolescent years had a greater impact on whether or not they were arrested.

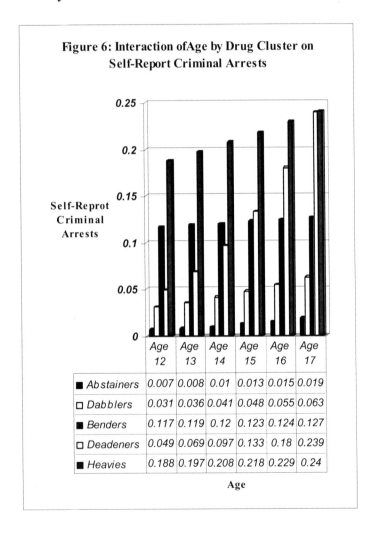

Figure 6: Interaction of Age by Drug Cluster on Self-Report Criminal Arrests

	Age 12	Age 13	Age 14	Age 15	Age 16	Age 17
■ Abstainers	0.007	0.008	0.01	0.013	0.015	0.019
□ Dabblers	0.031	0.036	0.041	0.048	0.055	0.063
■ Benders	0.117	0.119	0.12	0.123	0.124	0.127
□ Deadeners	0.049	0.069	0.097	0.133	0.18	0.239
■ Heavies	0.188	0.197	0.208	0.218	0.229	0.24

Older deadeners and heavyweights a have higher likelihood of being arrested for crimes than benders.

The 2001 NHSDA was cross-sectional, so inferences about causation over time were difficult to examine. These results neither supported nor refuted the life-course perspective especially because the model Chi-square did not change significantly between sets one and two. Once again, adolescents who were in one of the four drug using categories were more likely to report being arrested for crimes than abstainers, and each category of heavier use was more prone to arrests than other clusters. For arrests, the statistically significant differences between age and drug use cluster on arrests existed only in the heavy use groups (benders, deadeners, and heavyweights), who were likely to be life-course-persistent adolescents anyway.

Versatility of Criminal Activity
Criminal versatility was measured as a ratio-level measure. The NHSDA asked adolescents about six types of crimes they had committed over the past year. Regardless of the severity of crime, they received one point for each type of crime. If they committed zero crimes, then they received a score of zero. If they committed one type of crime, they received a score of one. Again, this process was repeated through all six types of crime. The measure was skewed, so to fit the assumption of normality, the scores were logged (base 10) (Tabachnick and Fidell, 1996). Ordinary least squares regression was the best standard analytic technique for this measure because it assumed a ratio-level dependent variable.

Using the same procedures as with the other two measures of crime, the results of versatility were presented in Tables 34 through 38 (Appendix E). Once again, the background variable co-efficients were identical throughout sets one of Tables 34 through 38, as they were controlling for each other and the clusters in the same fashion, regardless of which drug use group was omitted. Age (b=-0.010) was inversely correlated with criminal versatility, so younger adolescents were more likely than older ones to commit a wide range of crimes. Males (b=0.045) were more likely than females to be versatile in their crimes. Those who received income subsidies (b=0.029) were more likely to be versatile criminals than those who did not receive financial assistance. Finally, when compared to non-Hispanic whites, African-Americans (b=0.050), Native Americans (b=0.041), adolescents of multiple races (b=0.028), and Hispanics (b=0.022) were all significantly more likely to be versatile criminals. As in other measures, no difference between non-Hispanic whites and Asian-Americans existed.

In Table 34, abstainers were the omitted category. Dabblers (b=0.090), benders (b=0.212), deadeners (b=0.251), and heavyweights (b=0.312) were significantly more likely to be versatile criminals than abstainers. In Table 35, dabblers were the omitted category. Benders (b=0.122), deadeners (b=0.161), and heavyweights (b=0.222) were significantly more likely to be versatile criminals than dabblers. When benders were the omitted category (Table 23), deadeners (b=0.039) and heavyweights (b=0.100) were significantly more likely to be versatile criminals than abstainers. Finally, in Table 37 deadeners were the omitted category, and heavyweights (b=0.061) were significantly more likely to be versatile criminals than deadeners. The Pearson R-squared was 0.133, so 13 percent of the variance in criminal versatility was accounted for by age, race, gender (male), income subsidies, and drug use.

Criminal Versatility and the Life-Course Perspective
The criminal versatility and the life-course perspective was examined in sets two of Tables 34 through 38 and Figure 7. When the age interactions were tested, the model Chi-squares between set one and set two of Tables 34 through 38 changed significantly, so the results of the interactions may be interpreted (Tables 34 through 38 and Figure 7). The least likely group to be versatile was the abstainers. Young benders could be considered highly versatile whereas older benders were moderately versatile. In fact, young benders were at the same level of versatility as heavyweights, but older benders were significantly less versatile than heavyweights. Young dabblers were moderately versatile, and older dabblers were significantly closer to abstainers in their versatility.

Once again, these data were cross-sectional, so change over time cannot be determined. These results supported the life-course perspective, however, which stated that life-course-persistent adolescents begin their offending earlier and committed more crimes than adolescent-limited youths (Moffitt, 1993; Moffitt, 1997). Adolescents who were in one of the drug use categories early were more likely to be versatile offenders than adolescents who were abstainers or who used drugs later. As would be expected, older dabblers and benders were less versatile than younger dabblers and benders, as they related to the abstainers, perhaps because they contained adolescent-limited youths.

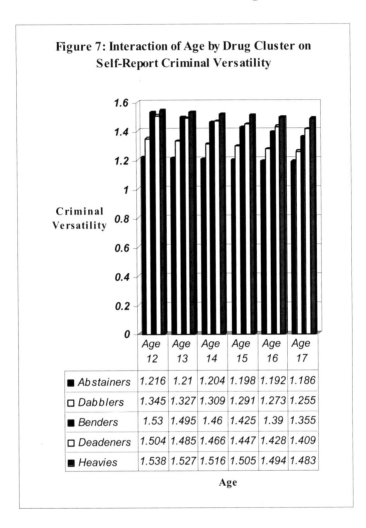

Figure 7: Interaction of Age by Drug Cluster on Self-Report Criminal Versatility

	Age 12	Age 13	Age 14	Age 15	Age 16	Age 17
■ Abstainers	1.216	1.21	1.204	1.198	1.192	1.186
☐ Dabblers	1.345	1.327	1.309	1.291	1.273	1.255
■ Benders	1.53	1.495	1.46	1.425	1.39	1.355
☐ Deadeners	1.504	1.485	1.466	1.447	1.428	1.409
■ Heavies	1.538	1.527	1.516	1.505	1.494	1.483

Age

Discussion and Conclusion

The third research question was: "Are certain clusters of adolescent substance use more likely to be associated with self-report criminal activity, criminal arrests, and criminal versatility than other types of clusters?" Throughout this chapter, the five types of drug users and how related to three different measures of criminal activity were explored. For the drug use clusters, each group demonstrated significant differences from the others in their likelihood of criminal behavior, and this phenomenon existed across all three measures of crime, aside from the deadener-heavyweight relationship, which only reached significance at the 0.10 level for self-report crime and criminal versatility. For the most part, substance use clusters consistently acted significantly from one-another, which was strong confirmation that palpable differences existed among them.

Prior literature found that the relationship between drugs and crime was significant and substantial (White, et al., 1985; Fagan, et al., 1990; Altschuler and Brounstein, 1991; McBride, et al., 1991; Thornberry, et al., 1993; Klein, 1995; Dawkins, 1997; Flannery, et al., 1999; Barrera, et al., 2001; Welte, et al., 2001; Bean, 2002). This relationship held true for the present research. In general, regardless of measure of crime, heavyweights were the most criminal, followed by deadeners, benders, dabblers, and abstainers respectively. The greater the breadth and depth of drug use within the cluster, the more likely adolescents in this group were to be involved in crime, regardless of measure. The strongest effect was that of the substance use groups predicting the criminal arrests measure, so more serious delinquents (hard substance users) were more likely to be arrested.

After an extensive search of the literature, it appears that no prior research examined types of heavy drug users and their correlations with criminal behavior. As will be discussed in Chapter 8, traditional measures of drug use did not distinguish among the three heavy drug use clusters examined in this book. Fagan and associates (1990), however, found that poly-substance use did not vary with increased delinquency, but extensive use of a single substance did vary positively with crime. The present research supported Fagan and associates (1990) because the dabblers, a group of poly-substance users, were significantly less likely than benders, deadeners, or heavyweights to commit crime, be arrested, or be versatile in their offending. Benders, deadeners, and heavyweights were all poly-substance groups, but their drugs of choice and the frequency of use varied among them.

Age was negatively associated with self-report criminal behavior and versatility, but it was positively associated with criminal arrests. Modest evidence suggests that the negative association between age and crime differed by substance use group. For example, the negative association between age and self-report crime and versatility was strong for dabblers and benders. These findings contradicted prior research that indicated that age and crime were positively correlated throughout adolescence (Hirschi and Gottfredson, 1983; White, et al., 1985; Blumstein and Cohen, 1987; Beyers and Loeber, 2003). Similar to these findings for versatility, prior research found that adolescents become less versatile as they aged (Beyers and Loeber, 2003).

Regardless of type of criminal measurement, males were more likely than females to commit crime. This finding supported results found throughout the literature (Hindelang, 1979; Thompson, et al., 1984, Osgood, et al., 1996; Sokol-Katz, et al., 1997). Once again, regardless of crime measure, those who received income subsidies were more likely than those who did not to self-report criminal behavior, arrests, and versatility. These results were consistent with those found in the literature (Shaw and McKay, 1942; Benda, 1995; Heimer, 1997; Matsueda and Heimer, 1997). Finally, African-Americans, Native Americans, adolescents of multiple race, and Hispanics were more likely than non-Hispanic whites to commit crime, be arrested for crime, and be versatile. Consistent with gender and income subsidies, these findings supported prior literature (Blumstein and Cohen, 1987; Sommers and Baskin, 1993; Sokol-Katz, et al., 1997; Flannerly, et al., 1999).

The fourth research question stated, "do the adolescent drug use clusters support the life-course perspective and the gateway hypothesis found in the literature?" Using multiplicative terms, the expected findings were that younger adolescents in the drug use groups would have a stronger relationship with crime than older adolescents in those groups. The age by drug cluster on criminal behavior interactions supported the life-course perspective (Moffitt, 1993; Moffitt, 1997). For criminal behavior and criminal versatility, young benders and dabblers had high rates of crime perhaps because these adolescents were life-course-persistent youths. Older benders and dabblers, however, had lower rates of crime as those groups could have contained adolescent-limited youths who were using substances.

CHAPTER 8

Clusters Versus Traditional Measures

In chapter 5, a cluster measure of substance use was introduced, which produced five distinct groups of adolescent drug users based on the substances they used and the extent of their use. In chapter 6, it was demonstrated that these clusters had unique relationships to background variables (age, gender, race, and income subsidies). In chapter 7, it was presented that the five drug use clusters related differently to three types of crime and deviance. In this chapter, a comparison between the 29 drug use measures found in the literature will be compared to these five clusters will be demonstrated. Of particular interest here is the extent to which traditional drug use measures are sensitive to the distinctions revealed in the cluster analysis. The final two research questions are: "How do adolescent drug use clusters compare with traditional types of measures of adolescent drug use found throughout the literature describing incidence and patterns of drug use?" and "Is the pattern of relationships in Figure 1 similar when drug use is measured by clusters instead of traditional measures?"

Researchers have used a wide range of methods to measure adolescent drug use. The 29 most common types of drug use measures were: individual drugs as dichotomous   measures, individual drugs as ordinal measures, an overall dichotomous measure, an overall ordinal measure, a sum of all dichotomous measures, report a sum of all ordinal variables, or a Guttman scale. The 2001 NHSDA reported 12 types of drug use, so 12 dichotomous, 12 ordinal, and five summary measures were created (Tables 26 and 27). Next, these measures will be compared against the drug clusters to examine the differences among them. Finally, to further examine these measures, their multivariate relationships between drug use and background variables and between drug use and criminal behavior differed by measurement strategy will be examined.

Traditional Substance Use Measures
In general, 29 substance use measures could be found throughout the literature. Many researchers maintained each drug as an individual construct (Wechsler and Thum, 1973; Hundleby and Mercer, 1987; McGee, 1992; Donnermeyer, 1993; Benda, 1995; Havey and Dodd, 1995; Graham, 1996; Andrews, et al., 1997; Bahr, et al., 1998; Ellickson, et al., 1998; Diego, et al., 2003). Therefore, a series of 12 dichotomous measures (one for each drug) and 12 ordinal measures were created. As for the dichotomous measures, 34 percent of adolescents reported using alcohol at least once during the previous 12 months (Table 7). Fifteen percent of adolescents reported using marijuana; seven percent reported using pain relievers; four percent reported using inhalants and hallucinogens; two percent reported using cocaine, tranquilizers, and stimulants; one percent reported using sedatives and methamphetamines; and less than one percent reported using crack and heroin.

TABLE 7: Range, Mean, and Standard Deviation Traditional Individual Drug Use Variables			
Variable	Range	Mean	S.D.
Alcohol (Dichotomous)	0-1	0.342	0.474
Marijuana (Dichotomous)	0-1	0.152	0.359
Cocaine (Dichotomous)	0-1	0.016	0.125
Crack (Dichotomous)	0-1	0.004	0.061
Heroin (Dichotomous)	0-1	0.002	0.048
Inhalants (Dichotomous)	0-1	0.036	0.187
Pain Relief (Dichotomous)	0-1	0.065	0.247
Hallucinogens (Dichotomous)	0-1	0.043	0.203
Tranquilizers (Dichotomous)	0-1	0.018	0.131
Stimulants (Dichotomous)	0-1	0.023	0.150
Sedatives (Dichotomous)	0-1	0.005	0.068
Methamphetamines (Dich)	0-1	0.008	0.089
Alcohol (Ordinal)	0-4	0.596	1.005
Marijuana (Ordinal)	0-4	0.343	0.943
Cocaine (Ordinal)	0-4	0.027	0.247
Crack (Ordinal)	0-4	0.007	0.127
Heroin (Ordinal)	0-4	0.004	0.092
Inhalants (Ordinal)	0-4	0.055	0.332
Pain Relief (Ordinal)	0-4	0.116	0.504
Hallucinogens (Ordinal)	0-4	0.064	0.345
Tranquilizers (Ordinal)	0-4	0.029	0.253
Stimulants (Ordinal)	0-4	0.044	0.330
Sedatives (Ordinal)	0-4	0.009	0.152
Methamphetamines (Ordinal)	0-4	0.014	0.187
n=17,429			

Overall, 39 percent of adolescents reported using any of these drugs (Table 8). Because 39 percent of adolescents reported alcohol use, the 11 other substances account for only a five percent increase. Therefore, adding more illicit substances to a dichotomous any/none measure of substance yields little information than that which was already present from a simple alcohol use question.

For individual ordinal measures of each drug, the range was zero to four, with zero designated no use and four indicating three or more times a week (Table 7). The mean for alcohol was 0.60, for marijuana (0.34), cocaine (0.03), crack (0.01), heroin (0.00), inhalants (0.06), pain relievers (0.12), hallucinogens (0.06), tranquilizers (0.03), stimulants (0.04), sedatives (0.01), and methamphetamines (0.01). Although these ordinal measures retained more information, the direct analysis required more interpretation than for dichotomous measures because the mean values were less intuitive.

The third type of drug use measure was an overall dichotomous measure of substance use (Novins and Mitchell, 1998; Keller, et al., 2002). In this study, 39 percent of adolescents used at least one of the 12 substances sometime during the past year (Table 8).

TABLE 8: Range, Mean, and Standard Deviation Traditional Scaled Drug Use Variables and Crime			
Variable	Range	Mean	S.D.
Overall Drug Use (Dich)	0-1	0.387	0.487
Overall Drug Use (Ordinal)	0-4	0.821	1.277
Overall Drug Use (Sum Dich)	0-12	0.713	1.237
Overall Drug Use (Sum Ord)	0-48	1.307	2.752
Guttman Drug Use Scale	0-3	0.616	0.906
Cluster: Abstainers	0-1	0.613	0.487
Cluster: Dabblers	0-1	0.314	0.464
Cluster: Benders	0-1	0.031	0.174
Cluster: Deadeners	0-1	0.020	0.140
Cluster: Heavyweights	0-1	0.021	0.145
n=17,429			

As stated earlier, this measure did not vary greatly from the dichotomous measure of alcohol use, making this method of measuring substance use even less desirable, so traditional measures with more variance are necessary to assess adolescent substance use.

The fourth type of drug use measure was an overall ordinal-level measure of substance use (Akers and Cochran, 1985; Cochran and Akers, 1989; Smart, et al., 1990). In this study, it ranged of zero (never) to four (two or more times a week), with a mean of 0.82 (less than once a month) (Table 8). For the most part, the overall ordinal variable represented depth of use because habitual use of one substance were placed adolescents into the highest level of use. The overall ordinal measure retained more information than the overall dichotomous measure and demonstrated more substantive breadth than the individual ordinal measures. Adolescents who often used one drug were categorized in the highest level of use for this measure, however it did not measure breadth of drug use. The overall ordinal measure contained five categories, each with at least 700 individuals. Therefore, it is an excellent measure for comparison against the clusters later in this chapter.

The fifth type of drug use measure was a sum (or average) of dichotomous substance use measure (Parker, et al., 1995). For this research, a sum measure was used. Both sum and average, however, are mathematically equivalent in correlation research. It ranged from zero (never) to 12 (each drug used at least once), with a mean of 0.71, so this was a measure more of breadth than depth of drug use (Table 8). In other words, this measure was a poly-substance use measure and did not provide information about frequency of adolescent substance use.

The sixth type of drug use measure was a sum (or average) of ordinal-level or ratio-level measures (White, et al., 1985; Marcos, et al., 1986; Downs and Robertson, 1990; Stice, et al., 1993; Kinnier, et al., 1994; Duncan, et al., 1995; Stice and Barrera, 1995; Harrison, et al., 1997; Flannery, et al., 1999; Kelly, et al., 2002). A sum of ordinal measure to replicate this method of operationalizing substance use was created. It ranged from zero (never) to 48 (each drug used at least twice a week), with a mean of 1.31, so this was a measure of breadth and depth of drug use. The mean was difficult to interpret, and the overall ordinal measure was the most ambiguous of the traditional substance use measures. Of the 49 levels of substance use within this measure, 15 had frequencies of zero, and 13 had frequencies of less than 10. Most of the adolescents' substance use patterns may be found in the first few levels of this measure, so it is skewed wildly.

Finally, the seventh type of drug use measure was a Guttman measure of substance use. The scale ranged from zero (no use) to three (use of at least one hard substance), with a mean of 0.72 (Table 8). The Guttman scales assessed breadth of adolescent drug use. The Guttman scale assumed hierarchical levels of substance use (Jobling and Snell, 1961; Robinson, 1973). In other words, if adolescents have used a hard substance, then the scale assumed that they have used alcohol and marijuana. This hierarchy did not hold true across all 17,429 adolescents. The scale received a Guttman co-efficient of reproducibility of 0.975 (Table 2), which was well above the appropriate 0.80 (Robinson, 1973). The Guttman scale assessed breadth of adolescent drug use. However, adolescents could have attained the highest level in this scale by experimenting with a hard drug, such as cocaine, but not using alcohol or marijuana. This scenario rarely happened as the Guttman co-efficient of reproducibility statistic demonstrated. Some researchers may be inclined to sum the dichotomous measures to attain a Guttman scale, to prevent the above scenario from happening, but this practice is incongruent with the Guttman scale assumptions (Robinson, 1973).

Agreement and consistency did not exist in the literature on the best method of operationalizing drug use. In Chapters 4 and 5, a cluster-analytic method was presented and compared those groups of users to background variables and three types of criminal behavior. The cluster drug use groups were compared against the drug use measures found throughout the literature to further investigate substance use measures.

Cluster and Literature Substance Use Measures
In this section, the drug use clusters developed in Chapter 4 will be compared against the drug use measures found in the literature. Additionally, a series of mean comparisons across substance use clusters by the 29 traditional measures will be created. The object is to see whether the clusters differ significantly from each other on the measures. In Table 39 (Appendix F), these differences were examined using Tukey's Honestly Significant Differences test. For example, in row four (crack) abstainers and dabblers were not significantly different from each other, so they were both designated with the subscript "a." The benders were significantly different from the abstainers and the dabblers, so they received a "b." The deadeners and heavyweights were significantly different from the other three groups but not from each-other, so they received a "c." For measures where all five clusters were significantly different from one

another, five different subscript letters were used (marijuana).

Overall, 290 mean differences using Tukey's test were compared against each-other. With five cluster groups and 29 traditional measures, a total of 580 combinations existed; half of these, however were reciprocals, so a total of 290 independent combinations were examined. No statistics were computed for the overall dichotomous measure, which suffered from complete co-linearity. All of the abstainers fell into the zero category and all of the dabblers, benders, deadeners, and heavyweights fell into the top category, and both were mutually exclusive.

Of the 290 combinations, 268 (93%) had means that were significantly different from each other (Table 39). Only for crack (dichotomous and ordinal) and the overall dichotomous measure were the clusters unable to differentiate substantively between users. The reasons were twofold: adolescents used crack with the second least frequently of the 12 independent measures (Table 1), and the overall dichotomous measure suffered from co-linearity.

The difference between deadeners and heavyweights was least strong in the previous chapter. However, on 20 of the 29 traditional measures, however, the deadeners and heavyweights were significantly different from each other. Overall, substantive and significant differences existed between the cluster groups on traditional substance use measures. In other words, the clusters deserve to be studied separately because their drug use patterns on traditional measures of substance use varied significantly.

The overall ordinal drug use measure and the Guttman drug use scale were particularly interesting because they produced categories that reflect the two dimensions, breadth and depth, that bookend the clusters well. Therefore, a series of cross-tabulations of the drug use clusters by these two overall drug measures were run (Tables 9 and 10 and Whiteford, 2004, Appendix F).

Cross-Tabulation of Overall Substance Use Measure and the Drug Use Clusters. The drug use clusters were compared against the overall ordinal drug use measure (Table 9).

TABLE 9: Cross-tabulation Comparing Drug Clusters to Literature Drug Measures: Overall Ordinal Drug Use					
Ordinal Category	Abs	Dab	Bend	Dead	Heavies
0.00	10,690 (100%)	0 (0.0%)	0 (0.0%)	0 (0.0%)	0 (0.0%)
1.00	0 (0.0%)	2977 (54.4%)	0 (0.0%)	0 (0.0%)	0 (0.0%)
2.00	0 (0.0%)	1486 (27.2%)	0 (0.0%)	0 (0.0%)	0 (0.0%)
3.00	0 (0.0%)	659 (12.0%)	80 (14.7%)	0 (0.0%)	0 (0.0%)
4.00	0 (0.0%)	348 (6.4%)	465 (85.3%)	351 (100%)	373 (100%)
Total	10,690	5470	545	351	373
n=17,429					

All adolescents who reported not using drugs were classified as abstainers and were exclusively in the no-use group of overall ordinal drug use measure. The dabblers, however, existed in all four ordinal stages of the overall ordinal drug use measure, but for the most part, the dabblers were classified as low users. The benders, deadeners, and heavyweights were classified almost exclusively in the high category in the overall substance use measure. Therefore, some dabblers were classified with heavy users.

The overall ordinal measure could not distinguish among the heavy substance use clusters (described above). An analysis of Tukey's Honest Significant Differences test demonstrated that mean differences did exist among the heavy use groups on almost all substances. The overall ordinal measure was an insensitive measurement that missed some clear and important differences in substance use patterns; differences earlier demonstrated to relate to significant differences in crime.

Cross-Tabulation of the Substance Use Guttman Scale and the Drug Use Clusters. The drug use clusters and the Guttman drug use measure were compared in Table 10.

All adolescents who reported not using drugs were classified as abstainers and were in the group coded zero of the Guttman drug use measure. All four substance use groups existed in all three levels of substance use within the Guttman scale, with the majority of dabblers in level one, and the benders spread equally across all three levels. Both the deadeners and the heavyweights were represented primarily in level three.

The Guttman scale measure exhibited several problems when compared to the cluster groups. First, it could not distinguish well between dabblers and benders and deadeners and heavyweights. Second, nearly 26 percent of the dabblers were in the highest category of the Guttman scale and were above 57 percent of the Benders, 35 percent of the deadeners, and 29 percent of the heavyweights. Finally, the highest percentage for the deadener and heavyweight groups was in the highest level of the Guttman scale.

TABLE 10: Cross-tabulation Comparing Drug Clusters to Literature Drug Measures: Guttman Measure of Drug Use					
Ordinal Category	Abs	Dab	Bend	Dead	Heavies
0.00	10,690 (100%)	0 (0.0%)	0 (0.0%)	0 (0.0%)	0 (0.0%)
1.00	0 (0.0%)	3598 (65.8%)	177 (32.5%)	27 (7.7%)	20 (5.4%)
2.00	0 (0.0%)	1401 (25.6%)	204 (37.4%)	130 (37.0%)	94 (25.2%)
3.00	0 (0.0%)	471 (8.6%)	164 (30.1%)	194 (55.3%)	259 (69.4%)
Total	10,690	5470	545	351	373
n=17,429					

In conclusion, three methods were used to compare the drug use clusters with the traditional substance use measures. The Tukey's Honest Significant Differences test demonstrated that ninety-three percent of the mean comparisons between cluster groups were significantly different on the traditional substance use measures.

The cross-tabulations showed that the overall ordinal and Guttman scale substance use measures could not distinguish among the drug use groups because the benders, deadeners, and heavyweights were categorized together. Analysis in the previous chapters demonstrated significant and substantive differences among the clusters' relationships, as well as its relationship with the background variables. Across the three types of crime significant differences existed in the comparisons among the three heavy-use groups. Because the overall ordinal measure and the Guttman scale of substance use failed to distinguish among the three heavy-use groups, they were less useful for assessing the relationship between drug use and crime. Furthermore, the dabblers were sprawled over several categories when compared to the overall ordinal and Guttman scale drug use measures. Therefore, even though the dabblers may be considered casual drug users with a weak relationship to crime, especially in older adolescents, the traditional substance use measures classified them across casual, moderate, and heavy drug users.

After using Tukey's statistic and cross-tabulations to distinguish among the cluster drug use groups and the two best traditional substance use measures, the substance use measures were regressed on the background variables and by crime measures to analyze research question five and see if substantive differences exist between the clusters and the 29 traditional measures of substance use.

Predicting Literature Substance Use Measures
The fifth research question states: "Was the pattern of relationships in Figure 1 similar when drug use is measured by clusters instead of traditional measures?" Throughout

this section, the 29 types of drug use measures found in the literature and their relationships to the background variables, age, gender (male), income subsidies, and race will be examined. These measures will be compared to the five cluster measures as well.

In Tables 40 through 42 (Appendix G), the regressions of each of the 29 traditional drug use measures found in the literature on the background variables were summarized. The b co-efficients were reported, using binary logistic regression or ordered logit regression, depending how the dependent variable was measured. For a complete review of each regression, please consult Whiteford, 2004, Appendix G. The ordinal measures were skewed, so to fit the assumption of normality, the scores were logged (base 10). For the sum of ordinal drug use measures, not all the values from zero to 48 had frequencies, so the variable was Winsorized to meet the assumption of a continuous variance. This process eliminated the empty cells but kept the ordinal rank of the data.

The strength of each measure could not be compared relative to the other types of regressions because the coefficients were obtained through different analytical techniques. However, to a compare of the direction and significance of each measure was applicable. The b coefficients from the drug use clusters using multi-nomial logistic regression were reported (Table 42). Only the coefficients that compared the abstainers with the other four drug use measures were reported because most substance use measures found in the literature have a zero or abstainer category.

Age.   Age was a significant predictor of all 29 measures, except for the dichotomous and ordinal inhalant measures (Tables 40 through 42 and Whiteford, 2004,

Appendix G). On no drug use measures were younger adolescents more likely than older ones to use substances. Therefore, regardless of drug or drug measurement, older adolescents used significantly more drugs than did younger ones. All four types of drug users in the cluster analysis were positively correlated with age, as well. Thus, older youths were significantly more likely than younger adolescents to be dabblers, benders, deadeners, and heavyweights than abstainers. These findings were consistent with the literature that stated older adolescents were more likely than younger ones to use substances (White, et al., 1985; Cochran, 1993; Benda, 1995; Duncan, et al., 1995; Stice and Barrera, 1995; Wood, et al., 1995; Andrews, et al., 1997; Akers and Lee, 1998; Bahr, et al., 1998; Parker, et al., 2000; Goode, 2001; Keller, et al., 2002). This relationship was so robust that it was found no matter how substance use was measured.

Gender. On the majority of drug use measures, boys were significantly less likely than girls to report higher drug use (17 of the 29 drug use measures). This included the most popular substances of alcohol, marijuana, and pain relievers, as well as overall dichotomous and the sum of dichotomous drug use measures. On no traditional substance use measures were boys more likely than girls to use substances (Tables 40 through 42 and Whiteford, 2004, Appendix G). The two best traditional measures, overall ordinal and Guttman scale of substance use, however, showed no relationship to gender (male). Contradictory to this finding, prior research using a variety of measures (ordinal measures of alcohol, marijuana, hard drugs, or overall ordinal measures) found that boys were more likely than girls to use substances (Wilsnack and Wilsnack, 1980; Cochran, 1993; Benda, 1995; Duncan, 1995; Osgood, et al.,

1996; Bensley, et al., 1999; Parker, et al., 2000). Other researchers found no difference between gender and drug use (Donnermeyer, 1993; Parker, et al., 1995; Stice and Barrera, 1995; Wood, et al., 1995, Andrews, 1997; Keller, et al., 2002).

The substance use clusters helped explain this apparent contradiction. The drug use clusters found that boys were significantly less likely than girls to be dabblers, but boys were more likely than girls to be abstainers, deadeners, and heavyweights (Tables 19 through 23 and 42). This measure demonstrated the complexities of examining drug use by gender, as it was the only one to show that boys used hard drugs more than girls. It supported the intricacies of the literature, as well. Some researchers found that girls started using substances earlier than boys and decreased their use less rapidly over time (Donnermeyer, 1993; Duncan, et al., 1995), which agreed with the finding that girls were more likely than boys to be dabblers. A substantial literature found that boys were more likely than girls to have a greater frequency of drug use and use harder drugs (Weschler and Thum, 1973; Wilsnack and Wilsnack, 1980; Cochran, 1993; Donnermeyer, 1993; Benda, 1995; Duncan, 1995; Osgood, et al., 1996; Bensley, et al., 1999; Parker, et al., 2000), which agreed with the finding that boys were more likely than girls to be deadeners or heavyweights. The relationship between gender and substance use was obviously sensitive to measurement strategy.

Income Subsidies. Those adolescents whose families received some type of government assistance were significantly more likely than adolescents whose families did not receive assistance to report higher drug use on 14 of the 29 drug use measures, including four of the five overall drug use measures (Tables 40 through 42 and Whiteford,

2004, Appendix G). On no drug use measures were adolescents who did not receive income subsidies significantly more likely than those who did to use substances. As for the drug use clusters, no differences existed between adolescents who received income subsidies and those who did not and their classification into a drug use cluster. For the most part, evidence from the majority of traditional drug use measures (15 of 29) and the drug use cluster groups supported previous research, which found weak relationships between measures of socio-economic status and adolescent substance use (Arafat, 1979; Hundleby and Mercer, 1987, McGee, 1992; Benda, 1995; and Parker, 1995). This relationship, however, was sensitive to measurement strategy

Race/Ethnicity (Compared to Non-Hispanic Whites). African-Americans were significantly less likely than non-Hispanic whites to report higher drug use on 25 of the 29 drug use measures, with the exceptions being hard drugs such as heroin (Tables 40 through 42 and Whiteford, 2004, Appendix G). On no traditional drug use measures were African-Americans significantly more likely than non-Hispanic whites to use substances. This finding was consistent with the drug use clusters, which found that African-Americans were less likely than non-Hispanic whites to be dabblers, benders, deadeners, or heavyweights.

Native Americans were significantly more likely than non-Hispanic whites to report drug use on only seven of the 29 drug use measures, but these were the most inclusive measures: sum of dichotomous, sum of ordinal, and Guttman Scale measures (Tables 40 through 42 and Whiteford, 2004, Appendix G). On no traditional drug use measures were Native Americans significantly less likely than non-Hispanic whites to use substances. As shown in

Table 33, Native Americans were more likely than non-Hispanic whites to be deadeners or heavyweights but no more likely than non-Hispanic whites to be dabblers or benders.

Asian-Americans were significantly less likely than non-Hispanic whites to report use on 20 of the 29 drug use measures. Exceptions were for hard drugs such as heroin and crack (Tables 40 through 42 and Whiteford, 2004, Appendix G). On no traditional drug use measures were Asian-Americans significantly more likely than non-Hispanic whites to use substances. Not surprisingly, Asian-Americans were less likely than non-Hispanic whites to be dabblers, benders, deadeners, or heavyweights.

No differences existed between adolescents of multiple races and whites and their use of drugs (Tables 40 through 42 and Whiteford, 2004, Appendix G), which could be due to the small number of multiple-race adolescents (n=332), making this comparison unstable. Similarly, as for the drug use clusters, no differences existed between adolescents of multiple races and non-Hispanic whites and their classification as dabblers, benders, deadeners, or heavyweights.

Hispanics were significantly less likely than non-Hispanic whites to score high on 16 of the 29 drug use measures, including the most popular drugs (alcohol, marijuana, and pain relievers) and four of the five overall drug use measures (Tables 40 through 42 and Whiteford, 2004, Appendix G). On no traditional drug use measures were Hispanics significantly more likely than non-Hispanic whites to use substances. As for the drug use clusters, Hispanics were less likely than non-Hispanic whites to be dabblers or benders, but no difference existed between

Hispanics and non-Hispanic whites and classification as a deadener or heavyweight.

The results of the traditional measures and the drug use clusters found here supported the literature that found non-Hispanic whites were more likely than African-Americans or Asian-Americans (Benda, 1995; Parker, et al., 1995; Wood, et al., 1995; Graham, et al., 1996) but less likely than Native Americans to have used substances (Wood, et al., 1995; Novins and Mitchell, 1998). These results contradicted findings that Hispanics were more likely than whites to use substances (Sokol-Katz, et al., 1997; Flannerly, et al., 1999). Once again, the relationship between race and drug use was robust. Relationships found to be significant using cluster analysis were likely to be significant using the traditional measures

Conclusion of Literature Drug Use Measures and Background Variables
Although the literature produced 29 methods to operationalize substance use, the relationships of drug use to the background variables of age, gender, income subsidies, and race/ethnicity was often not sensitive to different measurement strategies. Regardless of how substance use was operationalized, older adolescents were significantly more likely to use substances, both in breadth and depth, than were younger adolescents. As traditionally measured, females were generally significantly more likely than males to use substances. African-Americans and Asian-Americans were less likely than non-Hispanic whites to use substances. For the most part, adolescents who received income subsidies were more likely than those who did not to use substances. Hispanics were less likely than non-Hispanic whites to use substances, but Native

Americans were more likely than non-Hispanic whites to use drugs. No differences were found between non-Hispanic whites and adolescents of multiple races.

Although age and racial comparisons for the clusters were similar, coefficients for gender and income subsidies were different for clusters than for traditional drug use measures. Adolescents who received income subsidies were more likely to be classified as dabblers, benders, deadeners, or heavyweights, which is contradictory to the findings using other measures. In Tables 40 through 42, it was demonstrated that adolescents who received income subsidies were more likely to use drugs than adolescents who did not receive income subsidies. The most interesting finding, however was for the gender (male) in the cluster analysis.

On 17 of the 29 traditional measures, boys were less likely than girls to use substances. On the other hand, when substance use was measured by clusters, girls were more likely than boys to be dabblers, but boys were more likely than girls to be abstainers, deadeners, or heavyweights. This result demonstrated that females were poly-substance users, whereas boys were more likely to refrain from using substance use or to use them heavily. Neither prior research, which usually found that boys were more likely to use substances, nor the traditional measures used in this paper, which usually found that girls were more likely to be substance users, illuminated this gender pattern.

This unique relationship between gender and substance use by will be examined later in this chapter by creating a series of nominal-level variables from the two best traditional substance use measures, the overall ordinal and Guttman scale.

Predicting Criminal Activity, Arrests, and Versatility by Literature Substance Use Measures

In this section, the relationship between various drug use measures and their relationships to self-report criminal behavior, criminal arrests, and criminal versatility will be examined. In Tables 43 through 45 (Appendix H), the regressions of the three crime measures on each of the 29 drug use variables controlling for background variables will be summarized. For a complete review of each regression please consult Whiteford, 2004, Appendix H.

Self-Report Criminal Behavior

The 2001 NHSDA asked adolescents about six types of criminal behavior. If the adolescents had committed any of the six crimes, regardless of severity, they were coded one, and if they had not, they were coded zero. Therefore, self-report criminal behavior was a dichotomous measure. Thirty-two percent of adolescent reported committing a crime over the past 12 months (Table 1). At the bi-variate level, self-report crime was significantly correlated with all measures of adolescent substance use, including all 12 individual measures of both dichotomous and ordinal level variables of drug use (Whiteford, 2004, Appendix B).

Now, examining the multi-variate results, self-report criminal behavior was significantly predicted by 19 of the 29 traditional measures of drug use, including the most popular substances alcohol, marijuana, and pain relievers, as well as the five combined drug use measures (Tables 43 through 45 and Whiteford, 2004, Appendix H). Therefore, adolescents who used substances (or more substances) were more likely than those who did not use substances (or fewer substances) to commit criminal behavior, pretty much regardless of measurement.

For the drug use clusters, dabblers, benders, deadeners, and heavyweights all significantly predicted self-report crime. In this case, heavyweights had the strongest co-efficient (b=2.409), followed by deadeners (b=2.129), benders (b=1.799), and dabblers (b=0.945), with statistical significance differentiating across all of the clusters.

Both the traditional measures and the drug use clusters supported the literature, which found that adolescent substance use and criminal behavior were positively correlated (White, et al., 1985; Fagan, et al., 1990; Altschuler and Brounstein, 1991; McBride, et al., 1991; Thornberry, et al., 1993; Klein, 1995; Dawkins, 1997; Flannery, et al., 1999; Barrera, et al., 2001; Welte, et al., 2001; Bean, 2002).

One comparison among the traditional measures and the cluster measures in their relationship to self-report criminal behavior can be assessed by examining the Pearson and Nagelkerke coefficients. Using background variables and the cluster measure, 12.1 percent of self-report crime was explained (Table 46, Appendix I). Five of the seven traditional measures had slightly higher Nagelkerke explained variance (within 0.02 or 2%) (Table 46). Therefore, within these regressions, most of the traditional measures had a modestly higher explained variance than the clusters. On the other hand, the traditional measures used in this analysis were unable to distinguish among the heavy use groups, bender, deadeners, and heavyweights (Tables 9 and 10). This was an important distinction to make as differences existed among these heavy use groups as they correlated with self-report criminal behavior (Tables 24 through 28 and Table 45). This will be discussed further in the concluding chapter.

Criminal Arrests

The 2001 NHSDA asked adolescents about 17 crimes for which they may had been arrested and booked. If the adolescents were arrested for any of the 17 crimes, regardless of severity, they were coded one, and if they had not, they were coded zero. Therefore, criminal arrests was a dichotomous measure. Four percent of adolescent reported being arrested over the past 12 months (Table 1). At the bi-variate level, criminal arrests was significantly correlated with all types of adolescent substance use, including all 12 individual measures of both dichotomous and ordinal-level variables of drug use (Whiteford, 2004, Appendix B).

Looking at multivariate results, criminal arrests was significantly predicted by 14 of the 29 traditional measures of drug use, including the most popular substances alcohol and marijuana as well as the five combined drug use measures (Tables 43 through 45 and Whiteford, 2004, Appendix H). Therefore, on half of the traditional measures, adolescent substance users were more likely than those who did not use substances to be arrested and booked. For the drug use clusters, the drug use groups were all significantly correlated with criminal arrests and significantly different from one-another, so differences among the clusters can be explored. Heavyweights had the strongest co-efficient (3.027), followed by deadeners (2.694), benders (2.311), and dabblers (1.410).

Prior literature reported a significant and substantial relationship between drug use and crime. The relationship between traditional substance use measures, substance use clusters, and the criminal arrests measure yielded nearly identical results to the self-report criminal arrests measure. The co-efficients for both the traditional measures and the drug use clusters on criminal arrests were more substantial than for self-reported criminal behavior. In other words, the overall dichotomous measure had a b co-efficient of 1.123 with self-report crime and 1.738 with criminal arrests (both used same analytical technique so comparisons are valid). Once again, significant differences did arise among the benders, deadeners, and heavyweights when correlated with self-report criminal arrests (Tables 29 through 33), which cannot be detected by traditional measures of substance use.

Finally, Nagelkerke was used to estimate the explained variance of the drug use clusters with the traditional measures on criminal arrests. The clusters and background variables had an explained variance of 0.177 in predicting criminal arrests (Table 46). The traditional measures had somewhat higher Nagelkerke correlation co-efficients (0.183 to 0.202) for criminal arrests on all but three of the measures (Table 46). Once again, the traditional measures were moderately better able to explain variance in criminal arrests (0.025) than the clusters.

Criminal Versatility
The 2001 NHSDA inquired about six types of criminal behavior. Adolescents received one point for every crime they committed, regardless of the number of times. The responses were summed, and the adolescents received scores from zero to six (regardless of severity). Therefore, self-report criminal versatility was an interval measure. The mean was 0.52 (Table 1). At the bi-variate level, criminal versatility was significantly correlated with all measures of adolescent substance use (Whiteford, 2004, Appendix B).

Criminal versatility was significantly predicted by 22 of the 29 traditional measures of drug use, including popular substances, such as alcohol, marijuana, and pain relievers, and all five of the combined drug use measures (Tables 43 through 45 and Whiteford, 2004, Appendix H). Once again, adolescents who used substances (or more substances) were more likely than those who did not use substances (or fewer substances) to be versatile in their criminal offending. Interestingly, the dichotomous crack measure was inversely related with criminal versatility. Adolescents who used crack were significantly less likely to be versatile in their criminal offending than those who did not use crack. For the clusters, the substance use groups were all predictors criminal versatility and significantly different from one-another. In ascending strength, the clusters rank from dabblers (0.090), through benders (0.212) and deadeners (0.251) to heavyweights (0.312).

As stated above, prior research found that substance use and criminal behavior were significantly related, and significant differences among benders, deadeners, and heavyweights as they related to versatility existed here, as well (Tables 34 through 38). No prior research found that adolescents who use crack were less likely to be versatile. This strange relationship may be a casualty of a Type I error, or false positive, which will happen randomly in five out of every 100 tests (Kline, 1998). Finally, the traditional substance use measures and the drug use clusters supported the literature, which stated that adolescents were versatile in their criminal offending (Klein, 1984; Britt, 1994).

Once again, the Nagelkerke estimate of explained variance was used to compare the effectiveness of drug use clusters with the traditional measures in explaining criminal versatility. Along with the background variables, the clusters were able to explain 13.3 percent of criminal versatility; however the traditional measures were able to explain a somewhat greater amount of variance (0.134 to 0.157) than the clusters on five of the seven regressions (Table 46).

Conclusion of Criminal Behavior and the Substance Use Measures

Almost exclusively, adolescents who used substances were significantly more likely to commit crime, be arrested for crime, and be versatile in their criminal offending. This robust finding was virtually independent of measurement, for the most part, and the traditional measures had greater Nagelkerke explained variance than the clusters but by less than three percent on any given co-efficient.

The only major variation between the clusters and the traditional measures, as they related to background variables and the three measures of crime, was the difference in their findings between gender and substance use. The relationship between gender and drug use appeared to be non-linear, which did not exist with single ordinal (or continuous) variables without special treatment. Was this unique relationship between gender and substance use a product of the clusters or was it a function of the non-linear relationship between gender and substance use? To investigate further this substantively important relationship, which was evident only in the cluster measure, the two best traditional substance use measures were abstracted, the overall ordinal, a measure of depth, and the Guttman scale, a measure of breadth, and created a series of nominal-level variables, similar to the clusters.

Recoded Versions of the Overall Ordinal and Guttman Scale Measures of Adolescent Substance Use

The overall ordinal substance use scale and the substance use Guttman scale were recoded as a series of nominal measures at each level, identical to the way the clusters were coded, to investigate the unique U-shaped relationship between gender and substance use, which cannot be detected by nonlinear measures of drug use. Although no prior literature operationalized substance use measures this way, it allowed further explanation to be conducted to examine the relationships between the clusters and these two traditional substance use measures.

TABLE 11: Range, Mean, and Standard Deviation of Substance Use Guttman Scale, Overall Ordinal Substance Use, and Substance Use Clusters Predicting Self-Report Crime				
Variable	Range	Mean	S.D.	n
Overall Ordinal Level 0	0-1	0.613	0.487	10,690
Overall Ordinal Level 1	0-1	0.171	0.376	2,977
Overall Ordinal Level 2	0-1	0.085	0.279	1,486
Overall Ordinal Level 3	0-1	0.042	0.201	739
Overall Ordinal Level 4	0-1	0.089	0.284	1,537
Guttman Scale Level 1	0-1	0.613	0.487	10,690
Guttman Scale Level 2	0-1	0.219	0.414	3,822
Guttman Scale Level 3	0-1	0.105	0.306\	1,829
Guttman Scale Level 3	0-1	0.062	0.242	1,088
Cluster: Abstainers	0-1	0.613	0.487	10,690
Cluster: Dabblers	0-1	0.314	0.464	5,470
Cluster: Benders	0-1	0.031	0.174	545
Cluster: Deadeners	0-1	0.020	0.140	351
Cluster: Heavyweights	0-1	0.021	0.145	373
n=17,429 (per measure)				

The overall ordinal substance use measure consisted of five levels, so to make a new series of nominal measures, five overall ordinal-level measures were created (Table 11). Sixty-one percent were level zero (no use), the exact same group as the abstainers, 17 percent were level one (once a month or less), nine percent were level two (between once a month and once a week), four percent were level three (between once a week and two to three times a week), and nine percent were level four (more than three times a week) (Table 11). The substance use Guttman scale consisted of four levels. Sixty-one percent were level zero (the same as abstainers), 18 percent were level one, nine percent were level two, and 12 percent were level three (Table 11).

First, the relationship between the nominal-level overall ordinal and Guttman scales to the background variables were assessed (Tables 12 and 13 and Whiteford, 2004, Appendix I), and their relationships to the three measures of crime was also examined (Tables 14 through 16 and Whiteford, 2004, Appendix I). The similarities and differences between the two nominal series measures and the cluster groups will help further explain this unique finding.

The nominal overall ordinal substance use measures and the nominal Guttman scale substance use measures were regressed on the background variables using multinomial logistic regression (Table 12 and Table 13 and Whiteford, 2004, Appendix I).

The nominal overall ordinal and clusters (Tables 19 through 23) were related to age with the same number, direction, and level of significant relationships. For the nominal Guttman scale, however, older adolescents were more likely than younger ones to be casual substance users

TABLE 12: Binary Logistic Regression of Background Variables Predicting Overall Ordinal Substance Use

	O0 v O1	O0 v O2	O0 v O3	O0 v O4	O1 v O2
Age	0.410**	0.511**	0.608**	0.665**	0.101**
Males	-0.195**	-0.050	-0.184**	0.053	0.145*
Inc Sub	-0.067	0.088	0.169	0.305**	-0.155
Afr-A	-0.525*	-0.363**	-0.402**	-0.636	-0.162
Native	-0.117	-0.201	-0.261	0.534**	-0.084
Asi-A	-0.513**	-0.681**	-1.562	-1.220**	-0.168
Multi	-0.250	0.032	0.022	0.106	0.281
Hisp	-0.221**	-0.012	-0.258**	-0.164	-0.209*

	O1 v O3	O1 v O4	O2 v O3	O2 v O4	O3 v O4
Age	0.198**	0.255**	0.097**	0.154**	0.056
Males	0.011	0.248**	-0.134	0.103	0.237**
Inc Sub	0.236*	0.373**	0.081	0.218*	0.136
Afr-Amer	0.123	-0.112	-0.039	-0.273*	-0.235
Native	0.378	0.651**	-0.462	0.735**	0.273
Asi-Amer	-1.049**	-0.707**	-0.881**	-0.539*	0.342
Multi-race	0.272	0.356	-0.010	0.074	0.084
Hispanic	-0.037	0.057	-0.246	-0.152	0.093

n=17,429
**p<0.01   *p<0.05

but less likely to be hard drug users. Both the nominal overall ordinal and the nominal Guttman scale showed a moderate relationship with income subsidies, whereas the clusters had no relationship with this background variable. For race, the results among the nominal overall ordinal measures, the nominal Guttman scale, and the cluster groups were strikingly similar with the comparisons having about the same number, level, and direction of significant relationships.

	G0 v G1	G0 v G2	G0 v G3	G1 v G2	G1 v G3	G2 v G3
TABLE 13: Binary Logistic Regression of Background Variables Predicting Substance Use Guttman Scale Levels						
Age	0.480**	0.665**	0.442**	0.185**	-0.038*	-0.223**
Males	-0.140**	0.123*	-0.217**	0.263**	-0.077	-0.340**
Inc Sub	-0.073	0.205**	0.189**	0.278**	0.261**	-0.017
Afr-Amer	-0.620**	-0.094	-0.643**	0.527**	-0.022	-0.549**
Native	-0.516**	0.530**	0.364*	1.046**	0.880**	-0.166
Asi-Amer	-0.595**	-1.147**	-0.821**	-0.552*	-0.225	0.326
Asi-Amer	-0.286	0.122	0.065	0.408	0.351	-0.056
Hispanic	-0.178**	-0.082	-0.192*	0.095	-0.015	-0.110
n=17,429						
**p<0.01 *p<0.05						

The unique U-shaped gender (male) relationship with the drug use clusters was evident with the nominal overall ordinal measure, though not quite as clear as the clusters. As stated previously, boys were more likely than girls to be abstainers, deadeners, and heavyweights but were less likely to be dabblers. For the nominal overall ordinal measure, boys appeared less likely than girls to be low level users, but they were more likely than girls to be at the highest level of drug use. For the nominal Guttman scale, the U-shaped gender relationship with substance use was not apparent. Males were more likely than females to be marijuana users but were less likely to be alcohol or hard drug users because neither overall ordinal nor the Guttman procedure identified dabblers as a unique group.

Overall, except for gender, the nominal overall ordinal and the nominal Guttman scale measures acted similarly to the clusters when used as predictors by the background variables. The relationship between the nominal overall ordinal and Guttman scales and the three measures of crime were similar to the cluster groups, as well.

TABLE 14: Multi-Nomial Logistic Regression Comparisons of Overall Ordinal Substance Use, Substance Use Guttman Scale, and Substance Use Clusters Predicting Self-Report Criminal Behavior

	Omitted Category^				
	Level 0	Level 1	Level 2	Level 3	Level 4
	B	B	B	B	B
Omitted Category	Level 0	Level 1	Level 2	Level 3	Level 4
Ov. Ord. Level 0	-	-0.626**	-1.140**	-1.413**	-2.059**
Ov. Ord. Level 1	0.626**	-	-0.513**	-0.805**	-1.433**
Ov. Ord. Level 2	1.140**	0.513**	-	-0.291**	-0.920**
Ov. Ord. Level 3	1.431**	0.805**	0.291**	-	-0.628**
Ov. Ord. Level 4	2.059**	1.433**	0.920**	0.628**	-
Nagelkerke R^2	0.134				
Omitted Category:	Level 0	Level 1	Level 2	Level 3	
Guttman Level 0	-	-0.798**	-1.352**	-2.110**	
Guttman Level 1	0.798**	-	-0.553**	-1.312**	
Guttman Level 2	1.352**	0.553**	-	-0.758**	
Guttman Level 3	2.110**	1.312**	0.758**	-	
Nagelkerke R^2	0.124				
Omitted Category:	Abstainers	Dabblers	Benders	Deadeners	Heavies
Abstainers	-	-0.945**	-1.799**	-2.129**	-2.409**
Dabblers	0.945**	-	-0.855**	-1.184**	-1.464**
Benders	1.799**	0.855**	-	-0.330*	-0.609**
Deadeners	2.129**	1.184**	0.330*	-	-0.280
Heavyweights	2.409**	1.464**	0.609**	0.280	-
Nagelkerke R^2	0.121				

n=17,429   **p<0.01 *p<0.05

^Controlling for Age, Gender (Male), Income Subsidies, and Race

In Tables 14 and 15, a series of binary logistic regressions were run to analyze the relationships of self-report criminal behavior, and criminal arrests, to the nominal levels of the overall ordinal substance use measure and the Guttman scale of substance use.

TABLE 15: Multi-Nomial Logistic Regression Comparisons Overall Ordinal Substance Use, Substance Use Guttman Scale, and Substance Use Clusters Predicting Self-Report Criminal Arrests					
	Omitted Category^				
	Level 0	Level 1	Level 2	Level 3	Level 4
	B	B	B	B	B
Omitted Category	Level 0	Level 1	Level 2	Level 3	Level 4
Ov. Ord. Level 0	-	-0.960**	-1.531**	-1.797**	-2.654**
Ov. Ord. Level 1	0.960**	-	-0.571**	-0.837**	-1.694**
Ov. Ord. Level 2	1.531**	0.571**	-	-0.266**	-1.123**
Ov. Ord. Level 3	1.797**	0.837**	0.266**	-	-0.857**
Ov. Ord. Level 4	2.654**	1.694**	1.123**	0.857**	-
Nagelkerke R^2	0.186				
Omitted Category:	Level 0	Level 1	Level 2	Level 3	
Guttman Level 0	-	-1.149 **	-1.926**	-2.831**	
Guttman Level 1	1.149 **	-	-0.777**	-1.682**	
Guttman Level 2	1.926**	0.777**	-	-0.905**	
Guttman Level 3	2.831**	1.682**	0.905**	-	
Nagelkerke R^2	0.183				
Omitted Category:	Abstainers	Dabblers	Benders	Deadeners	Heavies
Abstainers	-	-1.410**	-2.311 **	-2.694**	-3.027**
Dabblers	1.410**	-	-0.901**	-1.284**	-1.617**
Benders	2.311**	0.901**	-	-0.383*	-0.716**
Deadeners	2.694**	1.284**	0.383*	-	-0.333
Heavyweights	3.027**	1.617**	0.716**	0.333	-
Nagelkerke R^2	0.177				
n=17,429 **p<0.01 *p<0.05					
^Controlling for Age, Gender (Males), Income Subsidies, and Race					

In Table 16, a parallel analysis of criminal versatility using ordinary least squares regression was also run. For each measure of criminal activity, regressions with each level variable as the omitted category once were run (similar to the cluster groups in chapter 5). The same results of the criminal measures on the drug use cluster regressions for comparison was also included (Tables 14 through 16).

TABLE 16: Multi-Nomial Logistic Regression Comparisons Overall Ordinal Substance Use, Substance Use Guttman Scale, and Substance Use Clusters Predicting Self-Report Criminal Versatility					
		Omitted Category^			
	Level 0	Level 1	Level 2	Level 3	Level 4
	B	B	B	B	B
Omitted Category	Level 0	Level 1	Level 2	Level 3	Level 4
Ov. Ord. Level 0	-	-0.055**	-0.111**	-0.144**	-0.246**
Ov. Ord. Level 1	0.055**	-	-0.055**	-0.088**	-0.191**
Ov. Ord. Level 2	0.111**	0.055**	-	-0.033**	-0.135**
Ov. Ord. Level 3	0.144**	0.088**	0.033**	-	-0.103**
Ov. Ord. Level 4	0.246**	0.191**	0.135**	0.103**	-
Pearson R^2	0.143				
Omitted Category:	Level 0	Level 1	Level 2	Level 3	
Guttman Level 0	-	-0.073 **	-0.141**	-0.831**	
Guttman Level 1	0.073 **	-	-0.068**	-0.182**	
Guttman Level 2	0.141**	0.068**	-	-0.114**	
Guttman Level 3	0.255**	0.182**	0.114**	-	
Pearson R^2	0.132				
Omitted Category:	Abstainers	Dabblers	Benders	Deadeners	Heavies
Abstainers	-	-0.090**	-0.212 **	-0.251**	-0.312**
Dabblers	0.090**	-	-0.122**	-0.161**	-0.222**
Benders	0.212**	0.122**	-	-0.039*	-0.100**
Deadeners	0.251**	0.161**	0.039*	-	-0.061
Heavyweights	0.312**	0.222**	0.100**	0.061	-
Pearson R^2	0.133				
n=17,429 **$p<0.01$ *$p<0.05$					
^Controlling for Age, Gender (Males), Income Subsidies, and Race					

The results between the drug use clusters and the nominal levels of the overall ordinal substance use measure and the nominal Guttman scale, as they related to all three of the measures of crime, were nearly identical.

Regardless of substance use measure, the relationship between adolescent drug use and crime was remarkably robust. In nearly every case, harder use groups or levels were more likely to be involved in crimes than no or low use groups or levels. In fact, 29 of the 30 coefficients between nominal-level variables of the overall ordinal measures and criminal behavior, criminal arrests, and criminal versatility had the same direction and level of significance throughout the analysis. Similar to the cluster groups, significant differences existed across the nominal groups for the overall ordinal and Guttman scale. For the nominal Guttman scale, all 18 coefficients, across all three measures of crime were in the same direction and significance level as the drug use clusters. Finally, 28 the 30 coefficients between the drug use clusters and the three measures of crime had the same direction and level of significance (except two). Overall, the comparisons among the two nominal-level traditional measures and the drug use clusters were nearly identical across all three measures of crime.

In conclusion, the overall ordinal substance use measure and the substance use Guttman scale as a series of nominal-level, independent variables, using the same method incorporated to code the clusters to further examine the relationship between gender and crime and substance use was included. Using this method to explore the differences between the drug use clusters and the traditional measures, it was found that the overall ordinal and Guttman scale measures correlated similarly across background variables and measures of crime (to the drug use clusters), except for the unique U-shaped curve of the gender (male) and drug use relationship, which the traditional measures did not detect fully. Perhaps this suggests that a categorical drug use measure may be advantageous to continuous measures because, like the clusters, they meet the requirements of a good substance use measure presented in Chapter 2. In other words, they do not violate standard analytic techniques and they are manageable measures of substance use.

Discussion and Conclusion
Throughout this chapter, 29 traditional approaches to measuring drug use as found in the literature was examined. The drug use clusters were compared with the traditional substance use measures in their relationship to background variables (age, gender [male], income subsidies, and race), and to three crime measures (self-report criminal activity, criminal arrests, and criminal versatility).

The Tukey's statistical test of comparing the cluster groups with the 29 traditional substance use measures demonstrated that the clusters differentiated among the traditional measures (Table 39). Of all of the relationships among the cluster groups, the deadeners and heavyweights were the most closely matched when regressed on background variables and when predicting the three crime measures. The deadeners and heavyweights were significantly different, however, on 20 of the 29 traditional drug use measures. Furthermore, neither the overall ordinal nor the Guttman measures could not distinguish among the drug use groups (Tables 12 and 13 and Whiteford, 2004, Appendix F). In fact, in most cases, the benders, deadeners, and heavyweights were categorized together, even through these three groups were related differently to age, gender, race, and income subsidies and to the three measures of crime.

The literature measures of drug use presented problems with analysis. Some literature measures must be adjusted for analysis (ordinal), group heavy users with moderate to light users, and were awkward to interpret (sum of ordinal). Indeed, the five overall measures of drug use found in the literature failed to distinguish among hard drug use clusters, which had been found to be significantly different from one another when being regressed on background variables (Tables 19 through 23), or when used as predictors of the three measures of crime (Tables 24 through 28).

The majority of traditional measures and the substance use groups were remarkably similar in direction of relationship and strength when correlated with background variables and crime, except gender. Although researchers throughout the literature operationalized drug use using vastly different procedures, the multi-variate results were similar when the traditional drug use measures were compared against the background variables and the three measures of crime (examined earlier in this chapter). Therefore, the issue of measuring substance use was robust, regardless of operationalization strategy.

The only relationship which was dissimilar between the traditional measures and the cluster groups was that of gender and substance use. To examine this relationship further, the best traditional measures, the overall ordinal and the Guttman scale measures of substance use were recoded, which measured adolescents' breadth and depth of drug use, into a series of nominal-level variables comparable to the drug use clusters. For the clusters, boys were less likely than girls to be dabblers but more likely to be abstainers, deadeners, or heavyweights. The nominal overall ordinal substance use measures found a similar result, although it was not as clear. Boys were less likely than girls to be moderate users, but boys were more likely to be at the highest level of use. The nominal Guttman scale substance use measure could not detect this finding. Therefore, it is important to examine non-linear relationship using categorical data or a series of nominal-level measures. The gender-drug use finding was a strength of the cluster groups that could not be detected by the literature, traditional measures, or traditional measures altered to replicate the clusters.

Finally, the traditional measures usually had a greater amount of explained variance than the cluster groups (comparing the Nagelkerke or Pearson coefficients). Researchers prefer explained variance when comparing identical groups of independent variables on different outcome variables. In this study, however substance use was operationalized with many different methods of measurement. The Nagelkerke and Pearson coefficients are important when examining the model's relationship value (Lewis-Beck, 1980). Here, the examining the overall predictive power is addressed. The correlation co-efficients can be misleading and easily manipulated, as well (Schroeder, Sjoquist, and Stephan, 1986). In this case, traditional measures with the greatest range (sum of ordinal) or greatest variance, or between variables (12 independent ordinal measures), had the greatest amount of explained variance. These measures were not considered preferable methods of operationalizing substance use. For this study, the nuances among the clusters, at the expense of a greater number of clusters or a greater number of adolescents within each cluster, was preferable.

TABLE 17: Comparison of Nagelkerke and Pearson Correlation Coefficients			
	Crime^	Arrests^	Versatility^^
Cluster Groups	0.121	0.177	0.133
Dichotomous 12	0.131	0.133	0.145
Ordinal 12	0.139	0.200	0.157
Overall Dichotomous	0.098	0.142	0.093
Overall Ordinal	0.131	0.183	0.134
Sum of Dichotomous	0.130	0.194	0.137
Sum of Ordinal	0.140	0.202	0.151
Guttman Scale	0.117	0.167	0.118
^Nagelkerke Correlation Coefficient ^^Pearson Correlation Coefficient			

In conclusion, the results were generally similar for traditional measures, but statistical differences between the cluster drug use groups and the traditional drug use measures existed, as well. Drug use measures found throughout the literature failed to distinguish the traditional relationship between gender and drug use. For example, boys were more likely than girls to be heavyweights, while no literature drug use measure found that boys were more likely than girls to use substances.

CHAPTER 9
Research Implications

Throughout this book, cluster analysis was used to examine adolescent substance use and its relationship to background variables and three measures of criminal and deviant behavior. Employing Ward's method and squared Euclidian distance, adolescent substance users were grouped into five categories: abstainers, dabblers, benders, deadeners, and heavyweights. Twenty-nine alternate substance use measures found throughout the literature were created and compared results using these measures to those drug use clusters. The 2001 NHSDA sample of 17,429 adolescents was used to examine these issues. The size of this data set allowed the researcher to delve into the intricacies of adolescent substance use and how it related to background variables and crime. Throughout this project, six research questions were explored, which are organize here by summary through addressing each question in turn and then discussing the results.

Research Question #1
Do adolescents cluster into several mutually exclusive groups of drug users with varying degrees of breadth and frequency of drug use? In Chapter 4, Ward's method was used to cluster the groups based on 12 illicit substances: alcohol, marijuana, cocaine, crack, heroin, pain relievers, tranquilizers, sedatives, inhalants, hallucinogens,

stimulants, and methamphetamines. These 12 types of drugs represented over 100 different specific drugs. Ward's method minimizes within-group variance and maximizes between-group variance (Ward, 1963). Along with the Ward's method, the average-linkage, complete-linkage, and single-linkage clustering methods were explored to distinguish among adolescent substance users, but the groups had low frequencies (less than 100) and little variation among the clusters.

Overall, five adolescent substance use clusters emerged. The abstainers were group one with 10,690 adolescents. Adolescents in this group had not used any of the 12 substances. The dabblers were group two with 5,470 adolescents. Adolescents in this group used many drugs but averaged using alcohol on 15 days over the past year, but no other drug averaged more than four days. The remaining 1,269 cases split into three groups of heavier users: benders, deadeners, and heavyweights. The benders (n=545) used alcohol on an average of 154 days per year, more than any of the drug use groups and had elevated substance use on the other eleven substances when compared to the dabblers. The deadeners (n=351) used pain relievers, such as Oxycontin, on average 40 days, which was the highest average of any drug harder than marijuana in any of the groups, alcohol on 70 days, and marijuana on 159 days. Finally, the heavyweights (n=373) averaged the highest rates of use on eight of the 12 substances, including using alcohol on 101 days and marijuana on 301 days.

In each cluster, evidence of versatility existed. In other words, adolescents who use one substance may use other substances. Indeed, in all four groups where adolescents reported use (dabblers, benders, deadeners, and heavyweights), each of the 12 drugs were used by at least one individual in the group. In other words, no substance use group contained patterns of individual use with only a few particular types of substances, such as alcohol, heroin, and hallucinogens.

The substance use groups had four distinct advantages over traditional substance use measures commonly found in the literature. First, the cluster groups used ratio data of 0-365 (days per year) on 12 substance use variables. Unlike traditional measures, the data were complete and did not have to be modified for use as a measure. Second, the data were nominal in nature because they formed groups based on person-centered data and not variable-centered data (Muthen and Muthen, 2000). Because the clusters are nominal-level data, they could be compared against each other when examining background variables or measures of crime. Third, the groups did not violate two common assumptions of standard analytical techniques, which were the assumption of continuous data and the assumption of a normal distribution (Fox, 1997). Therefore, the cluster groups were holistic, did not require modification, and did not violate assumptions of regression. Fourth, unlike almost all traditional measures, they included both breadth and depth of adolescent substance use.

Therefore, adolescents do indeed cluster into several mutually exclusive groups of drug users with varying degrees of breadth and frequency of drug use.

Research Question #2
How do the adolescent drug use clusters associate with background characteristics, age, gender, race, and income subsidies? Younger adolescents were significantly more likely than older ones to be abstainers, while older

adolescents were significantly more likely to be dabblers, benders, deadeners, and heavyweights. This finding was consistent with the literature that found that older adolescents were more likely than younger ones to be involved in drug use (White, et al., 1985; Cochran, 1993; Benda, 1995; Duncan, et al., 1995; Stice and Barrera, 1995; Wood, et al., 1995; Andrews, et al., 1997; Akers and Lee, 1998; Bahr, et al., 1998; Parker, et al., 2000; Goode, 2001; Keller, et al., 2002; Ford, 2005).

Females were significantly more likely than males to be dabblers, but males were significantly more likely than females to be abstainers, deadeners, or heavyweights. The literature on this issue was inconsistent, but cluster analysis may help disentangle this phenomenon. The cluster-analytic finding that girls were more likely than boys to be dabblers supported prior research by Duncan and associates (1995). The finding that boys were more likely than girls to be in a heavy use groups supported a large literature that found that boys were more likely to use substances (Wilsnack and Wilsnack, 1980; Cochran, 1993; Benda, 1995; Duncan, et al., 1995; Osgood, et al., 1996; Bensley, et al., 1999; Parker, et al., 2000; Simons-Morton and Chen, 2006). The explanation for this inconsistency in the literature may have been the unique U-shaped relationship of gender to the clusters use groups. Boys were more likely than girls to either not use substances or be heavy users, whereas boys were less likely than girls to use substances casually.

No significant difference existed between drug use groups and those whose families received subsidies and those whose families did not. This finding was consistent with previous research that found no differences among socio-economic status and substance use (Arafat, 1979;

Hundleby and Mercer, 1987; McGee, 1992; Benda, 1995; Parker, et al., 1995).

As for race, Native Americans were significantly more likely than non-Hispanic whites to be classified in a heavy use group, and African-Americans, Asian-Americans, and Hispanics were less likely than non-Hispanic whites to be classified in a heavy use group. Once again, this was consistent with prior research, which found that Native Americans were significantly more likely non-Hispanic whites to use substances (Wood, et al., 1995; Novins and Mitchell, 1998), and adolescents of other races were significantly less likely than non-Hispanic whites to use substances (Benda, 1995; Parker, et al., 1995; Wood, et al., 1995; Graham, et al., 1996; Novins and Mitchell, 1998), or no racial difference existed (Ford, 2005).

Thus, the adolescent drug use clusters did indeed associate with background characteristics, age, gender, race, and income subsidies. The findings were similar to those found in the literature, except for the gender-drug use relationship.

Research Question #3
Are certain clusters of adolescent substance use more likely to be associated with self-report criminal activity, criminal arrests, and criminal versatility than other clusters? Regardless of which measure of crime was examined, significant variation existed among the five substance use groups. This finding supported prior research, which stated that the relationship between adolescent substance use and criminal and deviant behavior was significant and substantial (White, et al., 1985; Fagan, et al., 1990; Altschuler and Brounstein, 1991; McBride, et al., 1991; Thornberry, et al., 1993; Klein, 1995; Dawkins, 1997;

Flannery, et al., 1999; Barrera, et al., 2001; Welte, et al., 2001; Bean, 2002; Weltem et al., 2005), although the causal process was unclear (Fagan, et al., 1990; Altschuler and Brounstein, 1991; Bean, 2002).

Not surprisingly, adolescents in the three heavy use groups were significantly more likely than abstainers or dabblers to commit crime, and dabblers were significantly more likely than abstainers to be involved in crime. What deserves special attention is the fact that significant differences existed among the three heavy use groups. As was discussed in Chapter 7, traditional measures of adolescent substance use commonly found in the literature could not distinguish among the three heavy use groups found here, and the traditional measures could not classify dabblers.

The clusters predicted criminal arrests more strongly than for the self-report criminal behavior and versatility measures because, perhaps, adolescents who were arrested were more likely to be perpetual criminals. Furthermore, the heavy use groups were more likely than either the dabblers or the abstainers, and the dabblers were more likely than the abstainers, to be versatile in their criminal behavior.

Therefore, certain clusters of adolescent substance use were indeed more likely to be associated with self-report criminal activity, criminal arrests, and criminal versatility than other types of clusters. In fact, the strongest evidence that clusters were robust was that on all three measures of crime, benders, deadeners, and heavyweights varied significantly from each other. Heavyweights were more likely than benders or deadeners to commit crime, and deadeners were more likely than benders to be involved in crime. Therefore, these findings demonstrate the need to examine different categories of hard substance users, rather than grouping them together as traditional measures tended to do.

Research Question #4

Do the adolescent drug use clusters support the life-course perspective and the gateway hypothesis found in the literature? Adolescent substance users may be classified in one of two types of criminal and drug user: adolescent-limited and life-course-persistent (Moffitt, 1993; Moffitt, 1997). Those who are adolescent-limited take fewer drugs and commit fewer crimes than life-course-persistent adolescents. Life-course-persistent adolescents start their delinquency earlier, and end later, than adolescent-limited youths (Moffitt, 1993; Moffitt, 1997).

In Chapter 7, the life-course perspective was explored. Longitudinal data is best suited to examine this theory, however the 2001 NHSDA is cross-sectional, thus conclusions must be viewed with caution. Overall, the self-report criminal behavior and the criminal versatility measures were congruent with inferences drawn from the life-course perspective. Although adolescents who were dabblers, benders, deadeners, or heavyweights were significantly more likely to commit crimes than abstainers, older dabblers and benders were significantly closer to abstainers than younger dabblers and benders. This relationship might be a consequence of adolescent-limited youths in older groups of dabblers and benders. Therefore, having been a dabbler or bender at an early age had a greater impact on criminal offending than being an abstainer. In fact, at age 12, the small group of benders (n=12) had the greatest percentage of criminal offenders compared to any other group, including deadeners and heavyweights.

For the criminal arrests measures, no significant differences existed between the abstainers or dabblers and the heavy use groups at any age. In other words, the differences among clusters and criminal arrests that existed at age 12 were similar at age 17. This demonstrated the stability of offending rather than change over time. The interactions that did exist were within the heavy use groups, who were most likely life-course-persistent adolescents.

In Chapter 4, the gateway hypothesis was examined, which states that adolescents who use drugs earlier in the life-course are likely to demonstrate a greater depth and breadth of drug use (life-course-persistent) than other adolescents (adolescence-limited) (Moffitt, 1993; Moffitt, 1997). Additionally, adolescent drug use follows a specific path through licit drugs, albeit for adults, to illicit drugs. Legal drugs, such as alcohol, were hypothesized to be a necessary but not sufficient step to using marijuana (Kandel, 1975; Welte and Barnes, 1985). This finding was supported by the Guttman scale as well. Although cross-sectional, adolescent drug use cluster data supported the gateway hypothesis. A greater number of dabblers, benders, deadeners, and heavyweights were older adolescents than younger ones. Heavy use groups were more likely than abstainers or dabblers to use alcohol and marijuana. Furthermore, within the heavy use categories, the majority of adolescents were age 16 or 17, so perhaps some adolescents who moved from abstainers to dabblers became benders, deadeners, or heavyweights. Thus, adolescent drug use clusters supported the life-course perspective and the gateway hypothesis found in the literature. To test this research question more directly would require panel data, which is longitudinal data of the same adolescents over time. This would allow the researcher to examine individual group changes across ages rather than making comparisons of older and younger adolescents within a specific drug use cluster.

Research Question #5

How do adolescent drug use clusters compare with traditional types of measures of adolescent drug use found throughout the literature in describing incidence and patterns of drug use? In Chapter 6, this research question was explored using a series of comparison tables.

Two methods were introduced to investigate these differences between traditional measures of substance use and the drug use clusters. First, the drug use clusters differ significantly from each other on nearly all of the 29 traditional substance use measures. Of the 290 combinations, 268 were statistically significant, suggesting that the drug use clusters represented separate patterns of substance use.

To delve into this comparison further, the two overall drug use measures were cross-tabulated against the five cluster groups. Both comparisons demonstrated differences between the clusters on the overall drug use measures. A few researchers used an overall dichotomous measure (Novins and Mitchell, 1998; Keller, et al., 2002), but this measure yielded no germane information as all of the drug use groups were categorized together. More researchers used a sum of dichotomous (Parker, et al., 1995) or sum of ordinal (White, et al., 1985; Marcos, et al., 1986; Downs and Robertson, 1990; Stice, et al., 1993; Kinnier, et al., 1994; Duncan, et al., 1995; Stice and Barrera, 1995; Harrison, et al., 1997; Flannery, et al., 1999; Kelly, et al.,

2002) drug use measures, but they required statistical manipulation and evaluation of content validity.

Some researchers used the overall ordinal measure to operationalize drug use (Akers and Cochran, 1985; Cochran and Akers, 1989; Smart, et al., 1990). For the overall ordinal measure, the three heavy use groups, benders, deadeners, and heavyweights were all represented together in the highest ordinal category (except for 15% of the benders group), so this measure did not distinguish among the heavy use groups, despite the fact that these groups varied significantly in their relationships to background variables and to the three measures of crime. Furthermore, the dabblers were represented in all four categories of drug use in the overall ordinal measure, so they were included with the occasional user, the moderate user, and the heavy user. The Guttmann scale measure yielded similar results as the overall ordinal drug use measure. The majority of dabblers, benders, deadeners, and heavyweights were represented across all levels.

Therefore, the adolescent drug use clusters compared favorably to the traditional types of measures of adolescent drug use found throughout the literature describing incidence and patterns of use.

Research Question #6
Is the pattern of relationships in Model 1 similar when drug use is measured by clusters instead of traditional measures? For the most part, the relationships were very similar whether substance use was measured by clusters or one of the traditional measures.

In the cluster analysis, older adolescents were more likely to be users; for 27 of the 29 traditional measures, older adolescents were significantly more likely to be drug users. The relationship between age and substance use was robust across measures. Females were more likely than males to be dabblers, but males were more likely than females to be abstainers, deadeners, or heavyweights. For 17 of the 29 traditional measures, boys were less likely than girls to use substances. The traditional substance use measures and the clusters differed substantively in characterizing the relationship between gender and substance use.

Both the cluster groups and the majority of traditional substance use measures found no significant difference existed between those who received income subsidies and those who did not and their substance use patterns.

Both cluster use groups and the majority of traditional substance use measures found that non-Hispanic whites were more likely than African-Americans, Asian-Americans, and for the most part Hispanics to use substances or be in heavy use groups, whereas Native Americans were more likely than non-Hispanic whites to be in heavy use groups. Therefore, the relationships of age, income subsidies, and race/ethnicity and substance use were robust regardless of measurement. The relationship between gender and substance use, however, differed dramatically based on drug use measure. Therefore, a series of nominal-level substance use measures were created from the two best traditional measures, overall ordinal, as a measure of depth, and Guttman scale, as a measure of breadth, to examine further whether this gender-substance use relationship was because clusters were sensitive to non-linear interpretation or because they combine both breadth and depth of adolescent substance use.

The overall ordinal and Guttman scale substance use measures was recoded into a series of nominal-level measures similar to the drug use clusters. The cluster groups showed a U-shaped relationship between gender and substance use where boys were more likely than girls to be abstainers and heavy users, and girls were more likely to be dabblers. The nominal overall ordinal substance use measures detected marginally this relationship. Boys were less likely than girls to be moderate users but were more likely to be in the highest level of use. The nominal Guttman scale substance use measures could not detect this unique relationship.

For all three crime measures, the cluster groups formed a significant ordinal ranking, which was, from least to greatest, abstainers, dabblers, benders, deadeners, and heavyweights. For example, the heavyweights were significantly more likely than the deadeners, benders, dabblers, and abstainers to commit crime, regardless of measure. This finding was similar to that of the 29 traditional measures. Self-report criminal behavior correlated positively with 19 of the 29 traditional measures of adolescent substance use, and criminal arrests and versatility correlated positively with 14 and 22 of the 29 traditional measures, respectively. A series of seven regressions for each of the crime measures was run on substance use, incorporating all 29 traditional measures (12 dichotomous, 12 ordinal, overall dichotomous, overall ordinal, sum of dichotomous, sum of ordinal, and Guttman scale). For each measure of crime, at least four of the seven substance use regressions had a higher explained variance than the cluster groups. A lower explained variance between the clusters and crime was a casualty of the relatively few numbers of adolescents in the three heavy use groups. Indeed, the relationships between the substance use variables and the three crime measures were remarkably robust, regardless of how the substance use measures or crime measures were operationalized.

Thus, the substance use cluster groups and the traditional drug use measures were related similarly to background variables and measures of crime. The differences were: (1) the explained variance, (2) subtleties among the benders, deadeners, and heavyweights as they correlated with crime, and (3) the gender-drug use relationship.

Discussion

The 2001 NHSDA reported that more than a third of adolescents aged 12 to 17 used illicit substances and nearly a third of adolescents committed crimes. The relationship between drug use and crime was significant and substantial (White, et al., 1985; Fagan, et al., 1990; Altschuler and Brounstein, 1991; McBride, et al., 1991; Thornberry, et al., 1993; Klein, 1995; Dawkins, 1997; Flannery, et al., 1999; Barrera, et al., 2001; Welte, et al., 2001; Bean, 2002; Welte, et al, 2005). The findings in this book established that this relationship between substance use and crime was so robust that it held virtually regardless of measurement strategy

Prior research, however, did not measure substance use consistently. Many different methods of operationalizing substance use existed, including individual and scaled measures, and dichotomous, ordinal, and frequency methods of operationalizing substance use. Cluster analysis is a sage alternative method of measuring substance use. It allows the researcher to maintain frequency level data on multiple substance use measures by categorizing individuals into homogeneous groups. The statistical demands of cluster analysis are similar to the methods used for traditional measures of substance use. Researchers can use cluster analysis on samples of less than 100 to over 20,000. At the present time, many computers cannot handle the amount of memory that is required to cluster-analyze a group of variables in a large heterogeneous sample. As computers become larger and more efficient, however this problem will diminish. The abstainers were removed before the cluster analysis was run, so this cluster analysis consisted of 6,739 adolescents using 12 variables. After the visual inspection that cluster analysis required, variables were constructed out of the groups created by the clusters. The extra time and effort needed to use this method over previous methods was minimal.

One of the primary issues with using cluster analysis is that it is difficult for other researchers to replicate one's clusters exactly. Each data set and each method of clustering will provide their own breakdown of clusters. In other words, unlike traditional measures, such as overall ordinal substance use, an exact method of constructing a replicated measure created by clusters is nearly impossible. In large heterogeneous data sets, however, the replication of cluster analysis should yield similar groups found here because the NHSDA was a representative data set of all incarcerated adolescents between the ages of 12 and 17.

Using Ward's method of clustering, adolescents in the 2001 NHSDA clustered into five mutually exclusive groups of substance users. As for many statistical procedures, several different clustering techniques exist for researchers. Along with Ward's method, between-groups linkage, single linkage, and complete linkage were explored, and none of these three methods were able to distinguish substance use groups that were large enough for interpretation. Ward's method clustered adolescent substance users into multiple numbers of groupings. In other words, Ward's method produced three, four, five, six, and seven cluster groups. Visual inspection of the data was necessary to decide the number of groups that was best suited for interpretation. Ward's method produced five groups appeared to be the best choice because the groups were large enough to run standard analytic techniques but were different enough from each other to be interpreted empirically. Therefore, the clustering method is part art and part science.

The designated five clusters were significantly different in their relationships with age, gender, income subsidies, race, and across the three measures of crime. This finding suggested that these five clusters identified using Ward's method were substantively meaningful and significantly different. The fact that three heavy use groups emerged in the cluster, which were categorized together by traditional methods of measuring substance use, showed that this clustering method was relevant and presented interesting findings. More importantly, however, was the finding that modest poly-substance use deserves special recognition and that the mere count of substances used may be seriously misleading.

For the cluster analysis measure to gain relevance, it must be compared to traditional measures within the literature. Using Tukey's statistic, most of the relationships among the drug use clusters across the 29 traditional measures were significantly different. In fact, the two most closely matched cluster groups, deadeners and heavyweights, were significantly different from one another on 20 of the 29 traditional substance use measures.

This justifies further analysis of the drug use clusters as a new measure of adolescent substance use.

The 29 traditional measures of substance use and the cluster use groups were remarkably similar when correlated with background variables and the three measures of crime, except for gender, which had a unique nonlinear relationship with drug use. Although the traditional measures varied in depth and breadth of substance use in nearly every case, the direction and strength of the relationship between the drug use measures and age, income subsidies, race, or crime were similar, demonstrating substantial robustness, regardless of how substance use was operationalized.

The most interesting finding was the relationship of gender to drug use. Males were more likely than females to not use substances and to be heavy users, whereas females were more likely than males to be dabblers or casual substance users. The traditional measures found in the literature and prior research failed to disentangle this relationship, except for the nominal measures of the overall ordinal substance use variable that detected marginally this U-shaped relationship between gender and substance use.

The theoretical implications for this U-shaped gender-substance use relationship are twofold. First, theories need to be able to explain the gender differences found in this research, boys were more likely than girls not to use substances or use them heavily and were less likely to be use substances infrequently. Second, gender and crime researchers need to discover whether this U-shaped relationship was unique to substance use or whether it existed for other types of crime. Furthermore, theories needs to be able to explain why this relationship does or does not exist across all types of crime.

The majority of traditional measures had a greater amount of explained variance than the clusters when used as predictors of criminal behavior. For two reasons, the differences in explained variance is not of concern. First, this study sacrificed explained variance for important subtleties among clusters. In this case, the two regressions with the greatest amount of explained variance were: (1) the 12 ordinal independent measures, and (2) the sum of ordinal measures. These regressions had a large amount of variance, which could lead to an inflated Nagelkerke or Pearson correlation co-efficients. Neither of these methods are outstanding measures of substance use. In this case, more nuanced measures, such as the clusters, are preferable to the traditional substance use measures at the expense of explained variance. Second, the greatest difference between the clusters and the traditional measures of substance use, and their explained variance when predicting crime, was 0.025, or between two and three percent of the total variance in the crime measures. This difference was not substantive enough to disregard the clusters.

Considering the 2001 NHSDA is cross-sectional, the results from cluster analysis were consistent with the life-course perspective and the gateway hypothesis. They supported prior literature, and they supported the theories because younger substance use groups were more strongly predictive of criminal behavior than older heavy use groups, perhaps because the younger substance use groups contained life-course-persistent adolescents and older substance use groups contained a larger number of adolescent-limited youths. For a more detailed analysis of the life-course perspective and gateway hypothesis, longitudinal data should be used.

Overall, the cluster-analytic method had four distinct advantages over traditional methods found throughout the literature. First, traditional methods frequently violated two assumptions of standard analytic techniques, the assumption of continual data and the assumption of normality. The cluster groups did not violate those assumptions because they were nominal-level measures. Second, all relevant information was maintained with the cluster analytic groups. The 12 substance use variables had frequencies of zero to 365, and these data were not altered to fit the assumptions of standard analytic techniques, so the measure was holistic. Third, cluster analysis yielded three heavy use groups that traditional measures, such as overall ordinal and Guttman scale, could not distinguish. The three heavy use groups were either categorized together (overall ordinal) or were all split across several levels (Guttman scale). Either way, the analysis of these three heavy use groups was difficult using traditional methods. Fourth, the clusters were able to distinguish the unique relationship between gender and drug use. Boys were more likely than girls to either not use substances or be heavy users, whereas girls were more likely than boys to us substances casually. The traditional measures did not demonstrate this relationship.

Conversely, the traditional measures exhibited four advantages over the drug use clusters. First, for drug use clusters using visual inspection of the data is vital, which is not necessary when using traditional measures of substance use. Massaging the data, however, may happen regardless of whether the drug use measures were found through visual inspection or statistical techniques. Second, although they could not distinguish among the heavy use groups within the cluster, the traditional substance use measures were predicted by the background variables and predicted the crime measures as well as the drug use clusters. In fact, the overall ordinal measure acted similarly to the drug use clusters when it was analyzed as a series of nominal-level measures. Third, on most of the crime measures, the traditional measures of drug use had higher estimates of explained variance than the drug use clusters. Finally, the cluster groups would be more difficult to replicate in other samples because the technique is open to interpretation, whereas traditional measures have a sequential pattern for researchers to follow when creating them. This does not mean, however that the clusters would not develop similarly using alternative data sets.

Regardless of the fact that traditional measures and cluster analysis were similar in their relationships to the background variables and the three measures of crime, clustering is arguably the best method for measuring adolescent substance use. The cluster-analytic method met all of the requirements for a good substance use measure (presented at the beginning of Chapter 2). It was a holistic measure that included an exhaustive list of all substances, over 100, measured in 12 variables. It was a precise measure because frequency data were used. Indeed, the clusters incorporated both breadth and depth into its measure of substance use. It was a manageable measure because it included only five groups, so it could be explored in small data sets. It did not violate the normal distribution or continuous data assumptions of standard analytic techniques. None of the traditional measures found within the literature met all of these requirements for a good measure of substance use.

The clusters were significantly different from one another in their relationships to age, gender, income subsidies, race, and the three measures of crime. The best traditional substance use measures, when analyzed as a series of nominal-level variables, found similar relationships to the background variables and crime, except for gender. The cluster analysis method demonstrated that both what substances adolescents' use and their frequency of use were important. This nuance demonstrated the differences among the drug use clusters, which allowed the unique relationship between gender and substance use to emerge.

Overall, this book had two primary strengths over previous research. First, as was discussed, it presented an alternative method for measuring drug use. Second, it examined 29 different substance use measures found throughout the literature. Few, if any, prior analysis examined and compared multiple substance use measures and their relationship to crime. The fact that the traditional substance use measures and the cluster use groups were similar in their predictive values and that relationships are robust is important for further research to consider when analyzing adolescent substance use. The series of nominal-level variables from the overall ordinal and Guttman scale substance use measures are good alternatives to the cluster analysis, although neither had been explored previously as a nominal-level variable.

In future studies, the substance use clusters should be replicated using alternative samples to determine whether the population of adolescents repeatedly groups into these five distinct clusters. The subtleties among clusters may lead to other interesting and substantively important findings. If researchers are unable to meet the demands of the cluster analysis, then they should measure substance use using a series of nominal-level measures from a measure of ordinal or frequency data or test for non-linear effects. An example of this method was the series of nominal-level overall ordinal substance use variables presented in Chapter 6. Unfortunately, however, researchers need to separate dabblers, which no alternative measure can do.

The consequences of not using cluster analysis are subtle but important. These consequences are not demonstrated in the robust relationships with the background variables and crime, but in the nuances of the measures that can detect important relationships that traditional measures might not find. A nominal-level measure of an overall ordinal or frequency measure will come the closest to meeting the requirements for a good measure of substance use. The nominal-level variables from ordinal measures of substance use demonstrated similar relationships to the background variables and the crime measures as the traditional methods of measuring substance use in prior research. The advantage of using a series of nominal measures is that they might detect small differences among levels of the variables or groups of the clusters.

A new method for measuring adolescent substance use and its relationship to background variables and three measures of crime was presented in this book. The measure met the requirements for a suitable measure of substance use and detected a previously unidentified relationship between gender and substance use. The NHSDA demonstrated that 38 percent of adolescents used substances and 32 percent committed crimes. This robust relationship was substantial and significant regardless of which measure of substance use or which measure of crime was incorporated. Future research needs to examine this relationship further and develop new measures and discover new subtleties.

Appendices

Appendix A: Drug Use Imputation

TABLE 18: Binary Logistic Regression Predicting Drug Use Imputation Dependent Variable: Drug Use Imputation			
	b	SE	exp(b)
Constant	-2.797**	0.250	0.061
Age	0.014	0.017	1.014
Gender (male=1)	0.115*	0.057	1.122
Income Help (yes=1)	0.266**	0.068	1.305
African-American	-0.103	0.088	0.902
Native American	-0.075	0.231	0.928
Asian-American	-0.018	0.165	0.982
Multiple Race	-0.134	0.219	0.874
Hispanic	0.060	0.083	1.062
Negelkerke R²	0.003		
Chi-Square	21.004	(df) 8	
n=17,429	**p<.01 *p<.05		
S.E. = Standard Error			

Appendix B: Background Variables Predicting Cluster Classification

TABLE 19: Multi-Nomial Logistic Regression Predicting Cluster Classification				
Omitted: Abstainers				
	Dabblers	Benders	Deadeners	Heavyweights
	B	B	B	B
Constant	-7.153**	-14.125**	-13.885**	-15.940**
standard error	0.167	0.529	0.627	0.671
Age	0.457**	0.756**	0.699**	0.824**
standard error	0.011	0.033	0.040	0.042
exp(b)	1.580	2.130	2.012	2.280
Gender (male=1)	-0.161**	-0.043	0.126	0.460**
standard error	0.035	0.090	0.111	0.111
exp(b)	0.851	0.957	1.134	1.584
Inc Help (yes=1)	0.040	0.193	0.256	0.320
standard error	0.045	0.111	0.132	0.129
exp(b)	1.041	1.213	1.292	1.378
African-American	-0.477**	-0.701**	-0.414*	-0.638**
standard error	0.056	0.155	0.178	0.183
exp(b)	0.621	0.496	0.661	0.529
Native-American	-0.012	-0.310	0.996*	0.710*
standard error	0.144	0.398	0.290	0.309
exp(b)	0.988	0.733	2.708	2.035
Asian-American	-0.675**	-0.927**	-1.749**	-1.629**
standard error	0.107	0.302	0.586	0.510
exp(b)	0.509	0.396	0.174	0.196
Multiple Race	-0.119	-0.277	0.161	0.540
standard error	0.130	0.351	0.372	0.302
exp(b)	0.888	0.758	1.175	1.715
Hispanic	-0.171**	-0.271*	0.117	-0.193
standard error	0.054	0.139	0.154	0.164
exp(b)	0.843	0.763	1.124	0.824
Nagelkerke R^2	0.184			
Chi-Square	2949.812**	(df) 32		
n=17,429	**p<0.01	*p<0.05		

TABLE 20: Multi-Nomial Logistic Regression Predicting Cluster Classification			
Omitted Cluster: Dabblers			
	Abstainers	Benders	Deadeners Heavyweights
	B	B	B	B
Constant	7.153**	-6.972**	-6.732**	-8.787**
standard error	0.167	0.533	0.631	0.835
Age	-0.457**	0.299**	0.242**	0.367*
standard error	0.011	0.034	0.040	0.042
exp(b)	0.633	1.348	1.273	1.443
Gender (male=1)	0.161**	0.118	0.287*	0.621**
standard error	0.035	0.090	0.111	0.111
exp(b)	1.175	1.125	1.333	1.861
Inc Help (yes=1)	-0.040	0.153	0.216	0.280
standard error	0.045	0.112	0.132	0.129
exp(b)	0.961	1.165	1.241	1.323
African-American	0.477**	-0.224	0.064	-0.160
standard error	0.056	0.156	0.180	0.184
exp(b)	1.611	0.800	1.066	0.852
Native-American	0.012	-0.298	1.008**	0.723*
standard error	0.144	0.399	0.291	0.310
exp(b)	1.012	0.742	2.741	2.060
Asian-American	0.675**	-0.252	-1.074	-0.954
standard error	0.107	0.307	0.588	0.513
exp(b)	1.964	0.777	0.342	0.385
Multiple Race	0.119	-0.158	0.280	0.658*
standard error	0.130	0.353	0.374	0.304
exp(b)	1.126	0.854	1.323	1.931
Hispanic	0.171**	-0.100	0.287	-0.023
standard error	0.054	0.140	0.155	0.164
exp(b)	1.186	0.904	1.333	0.978
Nagelkerke R^2	0.184			
Chi-Square	2949.812**	(df) 32		
n=17,429	**p<0.01	*p<0.05		

TABLE 21: Multi-Nomial Logistic Regression Predicting Cluster Classification
Omitted Cluster: Benders

	Abstainers	Dabblers	Deadeners	Heavyweights
	B	B	B	B
Constant	14.125**	6.972**	-0.240	-1.815*
standard error	0.529	0.533	0.802	0.835
Age	-0.756**	-0.299**	-0.057	0.068
standard error	0.033	0.034	0.051	0.052
exp(b)	0.469	0.742	0.944	1.070
Gender (male=1)	0.043	-0.118	0.169	0.504**
standard error	0.090	0.090	0.137	0.137
exp(b)	1.044	0.889	1.185	1.655
Inc Help (yes=1)	-0.193	-0.153	0.063	0.127
standard error	0.111	0.112	0.166	0.163
exp(b)	0.824	0.858	1.065	1.136
African-American	0.701**	0.224	0.287	0.063
standard error	0.155	0.156	0.229	0.233
exp(b)	2.015	1.250	1.333	1.065
Native-American	0.310	0.298	1.307**	1.021*
standard error	0.398	0.399	0.467	0.478
exp(b)	1.364	1.348	3.694	2.776
Asian-American	0.927**	0.252	-0.822	-0.702
standard error	0.302	0.307	0.651	0.583
exp(b)	2.528	1.287	0.440	0.496
Multiple Race	0.277	0.158	0.438	0.817
standard error	0.351	0.353	0.493	0.442
exp(b)	1.319	1.171	1.549	2.263
Hispanic	0.271	0.100	0.388	0.078
standard error	0.139	0.140	0.200	0.207
exp(b)	1.311	1.106	1.474	1.081
Nagelkerke R^2	0.184			
Chi-Square	2949.812**	(df) 32		
n=17,429	**p<0.01	*p<0.05		

TABLE 22: Multi-Nomial Logistic Regression Predicting Cluster Classification				
Omitted Cluster: Deadeners				
	Abstainers	Dabblers	Benders	Heavyweights
	B	B	B	B
Constant	13.885**	6.732**	-0.240	-2.055*
standard error	0.627	0.631	0.802	0.900
Age	-0.669**	-0.242**	0.057	0.125*
standard error	0.040	0.040	0.051	0.057
exp(b)	0.497	0.785	1.059	1.133
Gender (male=1)	-0.126	-0.287*	-0.169	0.334*
standard error	0.111	0.111	0.137	0.152
exp(b)	0.882	0.750	0.844	1.397
Inc Help (yes=1)	-0.256	-0.216	-0.063	0.064
standard error	0.132	0.132	0.166	0.177
exp(b)	0.774	0.806	0.939	0.938
African-American	0.414*	-0.064	-0.287	-0.224
standard error	0.178	0.180	0.229	0.249
exp(b)	1.512	0.938	0.750	0.799
Native-American	-0.996**	-1.008**	-1.307**	-0.286
standard error	0.290	0.291	0.467	0.393
exp(b)	0.369	0.365	0.271	0.751
Asian-American	1.749**	1.074	0.822	0.120
standard error	0.586	0.588	0.651	0.770
exp(b)	5.751	2.928	2.275	1.127
Multiple Race	-0.161	-0.280	-0.438	0.379
standard error	0.372	0.374	0.493	0.459
exp(b)	0.851	0.756	0.645	1.460
Hispanic	-0.117	-0.287	-0.388	-0.310
standard error	0.154	0.155	0.200	0.218
exp(b)	0.890	0.750	0.678	0.733
Nagelkerke R^2	0.184			
Chi-Square	2949.812**	(df) 32		
n=17,429	**$p<0.01$ *$p<0.05$			

TABLE 23: Multi-Nomial Logistic Regression Predicting Cluster Classification				
Omitted Cluster: Heavyweights				
	Abstainers	Dabblers	Benders	Deadeners
	B	B	B	B
Constant	15.940**	8.787**	1.815*	2.055*
standard error	0.671	0.674	0.835	0.900
Age	-0.824**	-0.367**	-0.068	-0.125*
standard error	0.042	0.042	0.052	0.057
exp(b)	0.439	0.693	0.934	0.882
Gender (male=1)	-0.460**	-0.621**	-0.504**	-0.334*
standard error	0.111	0.111	0.137	0.152
exp(b)	0.631	0.537	0.604	0.716
Inc Help (yes=1)	-0.320*	-0.280*	-0.127	-0.064
standard error	0.129	0.129	0.163	0.177
exp(b)	0.726	0.756	0.881	0.938
African-American	0.638**	0.160	-0.063	0.224
standard error	0.183	0.184	0.233	0.249
exp(b)	1.892	1.174	0.939	1.251
Native-American	-0.710*	-0.723*	-1.021*	0.286
standard error	0.309	0.310	0.478	0.393
exp(b)	0.491	0.486	0.360	1.331
Asian-American	1.629**	0.954	0.702	0.286
standard error	0.510	0.513	0.583	0.770
exp(b)	5.100	2.597	2.018	0.887
Multiple Race	-0.540	-0.658*	-0.817	-0.379
standard error	0.302	0.304	0.442	0.459
exp(b)	0.583	0.518	0.442	0.685
Hispanic	0.193	0.023	-0.078	0.310
standard error	0.164	0.164	0.207	0.218
exp(b)	1.213	1.023	0.925	1.363
Nagelkerke R^2	0.184			
Chi-Square	2949.812**	(df) 32		
n=17,429	**$p<0.01$ *$p<0.05$			

Appendix C: Background Variables and Substance Use Clusters
Predicting Self-Report Criminal Activity

TABLE 24: Binary Logistic Regression Predicting Self-Report Crime

Dependent Variable: Self-Report Criminal Activity
Omitted Cluster: Abstainers

	Set 1			Set 2		
	b	SE	exp(b)	b	SE	exp(b)
Constant	0.010	0.159	1.011	-0.398	0.203	0.672
Age	-0.116**	0.011	0.890	-0.087**	0.015	0.917
Gender (m=1)	0.433**	0.034	1.552	0.431**	0.035	1.539
Income Help	0.284**	0.042	1.333	0.283**	0.042	1.326
Afr-Amer	0.515**	0.051	1.683	0.512**	0.051	1.669
Native Amer	0.334*	0.133	1.403	0.331*	0.134	1.392
Asi-Amer	-0.149	0.107	0.859	-0.154	0.107	0.857
Multiple	0.333*	0.122	1.388	0.329**	0.122	1.389
Hispanic	0.246**	0.051	1.284	0.243**	0.051	1.276
Dabblers	0.945**	0.039	2.572	2.011**	0.351	7.469
Benders	1.799**	0.094	6.046	4.333**	1.202	76.137
Deadeners	2.129**	0.120	8.407	1.807	1.560	6.095
Heavyweights	2.409**	0.122	11.120	2.137**	1.708	8.475
Age*Dabblers				-0.073**	0.024	0.929
Age*Benders				-0.164*	0.076	0.849
Age*Deadeners				0.017	0.099	1.017
Age*Heavyweights				0.013	0.107	1.013

Nagelkerke R^2 0.121   0.122
Chi-Square   1568.338** (df) 12   1581.519** (df) 16
n=17,429
**$p<0.01$ *$p<0.05$

TABLE 25: Binary Logistic Regression Predicting Self-Report Crime

Dependent Variable: Self-Report Criminal Activity
Omitted Cluster: Dabblers

	Set 1			Set 2		
	b	SE	exp(b)	b	SE	exp(b)
Constant	0.955**	0.173	2.599	1.613**	0.287	5.019
Age	-0.116**	0.011	0.890	-0.160**	0.019	0.852
Gender (m=1)	0.433**	0.034	1.552	0.431**	0.035	1.539
Income Help	0.284**	0.042	1.333	0.283**	0.042	1.326
Afr-Amer	0.515**	0.051	1.683	0.512**	0.051	1.669
Native Amer	0.334*	0.133	1.403	0.331*	0.134	1.392
Asi-Amer	-0.149	0.107	0.859	-0.154	0.107	0.857
Multiple	0.333*	0.122	1.388	0.329**	0.122	1.389
Hispanic	0.246**	0.051	1.284	0.243**	0.051	1.276
Abstainers	-0.945**	0.039	0.389	-2.011**	0.351	0.134
Benders	0.855**	0.093	2.351	2.322	1.219	10.194
Deadeners	1.184**	0.119	3.269	-0.203	1.573	0.816
Heavyweights	1.464**	0.121	4.324	0.126**	1.720	1.135
Age*Abstainers				0.073**	0.024	1.076
Age*Benders				-0.091	0.077	0.913
Age*Deadeners				0.090	0.100	1.094
Age*Heavyweights				0.086	0.108	1.090

Nagelkerke R^2 0.121 0.122
Chi-Square 1568.338** (df) 12 1581.519** (df) 16
n=17,429
**p<0.01 *p<0.05

TABLE 26: Binary Logistic Regression Predicting Self-Report Crime

Dependent Variable: Self-Report Criminal Activity
Omitted Cluster: Benders

	Set 1			Set 2		
	b	SE	exp(b)	b	SE	exp(b)
Constant	1.810**	0.199	6.109	1.613**	1.185	51.161
Age	-0.116**	0.011	0.890	-0.251**	0.074	0.778
Gender (m=1)	0.433**	0.034	1.552	0.431**	0.035	1.539
Income Help	0.284**	0.042	1.333	0.283**	0.042	1.326
Afr-Amer	0.515**	0.051	1.683	0.512**	0.051	1.669
Native Amer	0.334*	0.133	1.403	0.331*	0.134	1.392
Asi-Amer	-0.149	0.107	0.859	-0.154	0.107	0.857
Multiple	0.333*	0.122	1.388	0.329**	0.122	1.389
Hispanic	0.246**	0.051	1.284	0.243**	0.051	1.276
Abstainers	-1.799**	0.094	0.165	-4.333**	1.202	0.013
Dabblers	-0.855**	0.093	0.425	-2.322	1.219	0.098
Deadeners	0.330*	0.145	1.391	-2.525	1.948	0.080
Heavyweights	0.609**	0.147	1.839	-2.195	2.069	0.111
Age*Abstainers				0.164*	0.076	1.178
Age*Dabblers				0.091	0.077	1.095
Age*Deadeners				0.181	0.123	1.198
Age*Heavyweights				0.177	0.130	1.194
Nagelkerke R^2	0.121			0.122		
Chi-Square	1568.338** (df) 12			1581.519** (df) 16		
n=17,429						
**p<0.01 *p<0.05						

TABLE 27: Binary Logistic Regression Predicting Self-Report Crime

Dependent Variable: Self-Report Criminal Activity
Omitted Cluster: Deadeners

	Set 1			Set 2		
	b	SE	exp(b)	b	SE	exp(b)
Constant	2.139**	0.212	8.495	1.410	1.547	4.096
Age	-0.116**	0.011	0.890	-0.070	0.098	0.932
Gender (m=1)	0.433**	0.034	1.552	0.431**	0.035	1.539
Income Help	0.284**	0.042	1.333	0.283**	0.042	1.326
Afr-Amer	0.515**	0.051	1.683	0.512**	0.051	1.669
Native Amer	0.334*	0.133	1.403	0.331*	0.134	1.392
Asi-Amer	-0.149	0.107	0.859	-0.154	0.107	0.857
Multiple	0.333*	0.122	1.388	0.329**	0.122	1.389
Hispanic	0.246**	0.051	1.284	0.243**	0.051	1.276
Abstainers	-2.129**	0.120	0.119	-1.807	1.560	0.164
Dabblers	-1.184**	0.119	0.306	0.203	1.573	1.225
Benders	-0.330*	0.145	0.719	2.525	1.948	12.491
Heavyweights	0.280	0.165	1.323	0.330	2.295	1.390
Age*Abstainers				-0.017	0.099	0.983
Age*Dabblers				-0.090	0.100	0.914
Age*Benders				-0.181	0.123	0.835
Age*Heavyweights				-0.004	0.145	0.996

Nagelkerke R^2 0.121   0.122
Chi-Square   1568.338** (df) 12   1581.519** (df) 16
n=17,429
**$p<0.01$ *$p<0.05$

TABLE 28: Binary Logistic Regression Predicting Self-Report Crime						
Dependent Variable: Self-Report Criminal Activity						
Omitted Cluster: Heavyweights						
	Set 1			**Set 2**		
	b	SE	exp(b)	b	SE	exp(b)
Constant	2.419**	0.216	11.237	1.740	1.696	5.695
Age	-0.116**	0.011	0.890	-0.074	0.106	0.929
Gender (m=1)	0.433**	0.034	1.552	0.431**	0.035	1.539
Income Help	0.284**	0.042	1.333	0.283**	0.042	1.326
Afr-Amer	0.515**	0.051	1.683	0.512**	0.051	1.669
Native Amer	0.334*	0.133	1.403	0.331*	0.134	1.392
Asi-Amer	-0.149	0.107	0.859	-0.154	0.107	0.857
Multiple	0.333*	0.122	1.388	0.329**	0.122	1.389
Hispanic	0.246**	0.051	1.284	0.243**	0.051	1.276
Abstainers	-2.409**	0.122	0.090	-2.137	1.708	0.118
Dabblers	-1.464**	0.121	0.231	-0.126	1.720	0.881
Benders	-0.609**	0.147	0.544	2.195	2.069	8.984
Deadeners	-0.280	0.165	1.323	-0.330	2.295	0.719
Age*Abstainers				-0.013	0.107	0.987
Age*Dabblers				-0.086	0.108	0.917
Age*Benders				-0.177	0.130	0.838
Age*Deadeners				0.004	0.145	0.996
Nagelkerke R^2	0.121			0.122		
Chi-Square	1568.338** (df) 12			1581.519** (df) 16		
n=17,429						
**p<0.01 *p<0.05						

Appendix D: Background Variables and Substance Use Clusters
Predicting Self-Report Criminal Arrests

TABLE 29: Binary Logistic Regression Predicting Self-Report Arrests

Dependent Variable: Self-Report Criminal Arrests
Omitted Cluster: Abstainers

	Set 1			Set 2		
	b	SE	exp(b)	b	SE	exp(b)
Constant	-7.378**	0.448	0.001	-8.018**	0.768	0.000
Age	0.160**	0.030	1.174	0.205**	0.053	1.227
Gender (m=1)	0.689**	0.088	1.992	0.689**	0.088	1.992
Income Help	0.421**	0.096	1.510	0.412**	0.096	1.510
Afr-Amer	0.493**	0.120	1.638	0.494**	0.120	1.639
Native Amer	0.589*	0.257	1.803	0.591*	0.257	1.806
Asi-Amer	-0.233	0.317	0.792	-0.235	0.317	0.791
Multiple	0.582*	0.257	1.790	0.560*	0.258	1.751
Hispanic	0.394**	0.117	1.483	0.395**	0.117	1.484
Dabblers	1.410**	0.113	4.096	2.241*	1.026	9.400
Benders	2.311**	0.164	10.084	5.216**	1.781	184.216
Deadeners	2.694**	0.171	14.794	0.178	2.285	1.194
Heavyweights	3.027**	0.159	20.642	5.233**	1.943	187.325
Age*Dabblers				-0.057	0.069	0.945
Age*Benders				-0.187	0.115	0.829
Age*Deadeners				0.155	0.145	1.167
Age*Heavyweights				-0.142	0.124	0.867
Nagelkerke R^2	0.121			0.122		
Chi-Square	1568.338** (df) 12			1581.519** (df) 16		
n=17,429						
**p<0.01 *p<0.05						

TABLE 30: Binary Logistic Regression Predicting Self-Report Arrests

Dependent Variable: Self-Report Criminal Arrests
Omitted Cluster: Dabblers

	Set 1			Set 2		
	b	SE	exp(b)	b	SE	exp(b)
Constant	-5.968**	0.472	0.003	-5.777**	0.667	0.003
Age	0.160**	0.030	1.174	0.148**	0.043	1.160
Gender (m=1)	0.689**	0.088	1.992	0.689**	0.088	1.992
Income Help	0.421**	0.096	1.510	0.412**	0.096	1.510
Afr-Amer	0.493**	0.120	1.638	0.494**	0.120	1.639
Native Amer	0.589*	0.257	1.803	0.591*	0.257	1.806
Asi-Amer	-0.233	0.317	0.792	-0.235	0.317	0.791
Multiple	0.582*	0.257	1.790	0.560*	0.258	1.751
Hispanic	0.394**	0.117	1.483	0.395**	0.117	1.484
Abstainers	-1.410**	0.113	0.244	-2.241*	1.026	0.106
Benders	0.901**	0.144	2.462	2.975	1.731	19.598
Deadeners	2.284**	0.153	3.612	-2.063	2.246	0.127
Heavyweights	1.617**	0.138	5.039	2.992	1.898	19.928
Age*Abstainers				0.057	0.069	1.058
Age*Benders				-0.131	0.110	0.877
Age*Deadeners				0.211	0.141	1.235
Age*Heavyweights				-0.086	0.119	0.918

Nagelkerke R^2 0.121   0.122
Chi-Square   1568.338** (df) 12   1581.519** (df) 16
n=17,429
**$p<0.01$ *$p<0.05$

TABLE 31: Binary Logistic Regression Predicting Self-Report Arrests

Dependent Variable: Self-Report Criminal Arrests
Omitted Cluster: Benders

	Set 1			Set 2		
	b	SE	exp(b)	b	SE	exp(b)
Constant	-5.067**	0.499	0.006	-2.802**	1.603	0.061
Age	0.160**	0.030	1.174	0.017	0.101	1.017
Gender (m=1)	0.689**	0.088	1.992	0.689**	0.088	1.992
Income Help	0.421**	0.096	1.510	0.412**	0.096	1.510
Afr-Amer	0.493**	0.120	1.638	0.494**	0.120	1.639
Native Amer	0.589*	0.257	1.803	0.591*	0.257	1.806
Asi-Amer	-0.233	0.317	0.792	-0.235	0.317	0.791
Multiple	0.582*	0.257	1.790	0.560*	0.258	1.751
Hispanic	0.394**	0.117	1.483	0.395**	0.117	1.484
Abstainers	-2.311**	0.164	0.099	-5.216*	1.781	0.005
Dabblers	-0.901**	0.144	0.406	-2.975	1.731	0.051
Deadeners	0.383*	0.191	1.467	-5.038	2.675	0.006
Heavyweights	0.716**	0.178	2.047	0.017	2.393	1.017
Age*Abstainers				0.187	0.115	1.206
Age*Dabblers				0.131	0.110	1.140
Age*Deadeners				0.342*	0.168	1.408
Age*Heavyweights				0.045	0.151	1.046

Nagelkerke R^2 0.121   0.122
Chi-Square   1568.338** (df) 12   1581.519** (df) 16
n=17,429
**p<0.01   *p<0.05

TABLE 32: Binary Logistic Regression Predicting Self-Report Arrests

Dependent Variable: Self-Report Criminal Arrests
Omitted Cluster: Deadeners

	Set 1			Set 2		
	b	SE	exp(b)	b	SE	exp(b)
Constant	-4.684**	0.499	0.009	-7.840**	2.149	0.000
Age	0.160**	0.030	1.174	0.359**	0.134	1.432
Gender (m=1)	0.689**	0.088	1.992	0.689**	0.088	1.992
Income Help	0.421**	0.096	1.510	0.412**	0.096	1.510
Afr-Amer	0.493**	0.120	1.638	0.494**	0.120	1.639
Native Amer	0.589*	0.257	1.803	0.591*	0.257	1.806
Asi-Amer	-0.233	0.317	0.792	-0.235	0.317	0.791
Multiple	0.582*	0.257	1.790	0.560*	0.258	1.751
Hispanic	0.394**	0.117	1.483	0.395**	0.117	1.484
Abstainers	-2.694**	0.171	0.068	-0.178	2.285	0.837
Dabblers	-1.284**	0.153	**xxxx**	2.063	2.246	7.870
Benders	-0.383*	0.191	0.682	5.038	2.675	154.006
Heavyweights	0.333	0.185	1.395	5.055	2.788	156.835
Age*Abstainers				-0.155	0.145	0.857
Age*Dabblers				-0.211	0.141	0.809
Age*Benders				-0.342*	0.168	0.710
Age*Heavyweights				-0.297	0.175	0.743
Nagelkerke R^2	0.121			0.122		
Chi-Square	1568.338** (df) 12			1581.519** (df) 16		
n=17,429						
**p<0.01 *p<0.05						

TABLE 33: Binary Logistic Regression Predicting Self-Report Arrests

Dependent Variable: Self-Report Criminal Arrests
Omitted Cluster: Heavyweights

	Set 1			Set 2		
	b	SE	exp(b)	b	SE	exp(b)
Constant	-4.351**	0.501	0.013	-2.785	1.778	0.062
Age	0.160**	0.030	1.174	0.062	0.111	1.064
Gender (m=1)	0.689**	0.088	1.992	0.689**	0.088	1.992
Income Help	0.421**	0.096	1.510	0.412**	0.096	1.510
Afr-Amer	0.493**	0.120	1.638	0.494**	0.120	1.639
Native Amer	0.589*	0.257	1.803	0.591*	0.257	1.806
Asi-Amer	-0.233	0.317	0.792	-0.235	0.317	0.791
Multiple	0.582*	0.257	1.790	0.560*	0.258	1.751
Hispanic	0.394**	0.117	1.483	0.395**	0.117	1.484
Abstainers	-3.037**	0.159	0.048	-5.233**	1.943	0.005
Dabblers	-1.617**	0.138	0.198	-2.992	1.898	0.050
Benders	-0.716**	0.178	0.489	-0.017	2.393	0.983
Deadeners	-0.333	0.185	xxxx	-5.055	2.788	0.006
Age*Abstainers				0.142	0.124	1.153
Age*Dabblers				0.086	0.119	1.089
Age*Benders				-0.045	0.151	0.956
Age*Deadeners				0.297	0.175	1.346
Nagelkerke R^2	0.121			0.122		
Chi-Square	1568.338** (df) 12			1581.519** (df) 16		

n=17,429
**$p<0.01$ *$p<0.05$

Appendix E: Background Variables and Substance Use Clusters
Predicting Self-Report Criminal Versatility

TABLE 34: Binary Logistic Regression Predicting Self-Report Criminal Versatility

Dependent Variable: Self-Report Criminal Versatility
Omitted Cluster: Abstainers

	Set 1		Set 2	
	b	SE	b	SE
Constant	0.186**	0.013	0.125**	0.016
Age	-0.010**	0.001	-0.006**	0.001
Gender (male=1)	0.045**	0.003	0.044**	0.003
Income Help	0.029**	0.004	0.028**	0.004
African-American	0.050**	0.004	0.049**	0.004
Native American	0.041**	0.012	0.041**	0.012
Asian-American	-0.011	0.028	-0.012	0.008
Multiple Race	0.028**	0.011	0.027*	0.011
Hispanic	0.022**	0.004	0.022**	0.004
Dabblers	0.090**	0.003	0.273**	0.031
Benders	0.212**	0.009	0.662**	0.103
Deadeners	0.251**	0.010	0.444**	0.135
Heavyweights	0.312**	0.010	0.382**	0.141
Age*Dabblers			-0.012**	0.002
Age*Benders			-0.029**	0.007
Age*Deadeners			-0.013	0.009
Age*Heavyweights			-0.005	0.009
Pearson R^2	0.133		0.135	
n=17,429				
**p<0.01 *p<0.05				

TABLE 35: Binary Logistic Regression Predicting Self-Report Criminal Versatility

Dependent Variable: Self-Report Criminal Versatility
Omitted Cluster: Dabblers

	Set 1 b	Set 1 SE	Set 2 b	Set 2 SE
Constant	0.276**	0.014	0.398**	0.026
Age	-0.010**	0.001	-0.018**	0.002
Gender (male=1)	0.045**	0.003	0.044**	0.003
Income Help	0.029**	0.004	0.028**	0.004
African-American	0.050**	0.004	0.049**	0.004
Native American	0.041**	0.012	0.041**	0.012
Asian-American	-0.011	0.028	-0.012	0.008
Multiple Race	0.028**	0.011	0.027*	0.011
Hispanic	0.022**	0.004	0.022**	0.004
Abstainers	-0.090**	0.003	-0.273**	0.031
Benders	0.122**	0.009	0.389**	0.105
Deadeners	0.161**	0.010	0.171	0.136
Heavyweights	0.222**	0.010	0.109	0.142
Age*Abstainers			0.012**	0.002
Age*Benders			-0.017*	0.007
Age*Deadeners			0.000	0.009
Age*Heavyweights			0.008	0.009
Pearson R^2	0.133		0.135	
n=17,429				
**p<0.01 *p<0.05				

TABLE 36: Binary Logistic Regression Predicting Self-Report Criminal Versatility

Dependent Variable: Self-Report Criminal Versatility
Omitted Cluster: Benders

	Set 1		Set 2	
	b	SE	b	SE
Constant	0.398**	0.014	0.398**	0.026
Age	-0.010**	0.001	-0.035**	0.006
Gender (male=1)	0.045**	0.003	0.044**	0.003
Income Help	0.029**	0.004	0.028**	0.004
African-American	0.050**	0.004	0.049**	0.004
Native American	0.041**	0.012	0.041**	0.012
Asian-American	-0.011	0.028	-0.012	0.008
Multiple Race	0.028**	0.011	0.027*	0.011
Hispanic	0.022**	0.004	0.022**	0.004
Abstainers	-0.212**	0.003	-0.662**	0.103
Dabblers	-0.122**	0.009	-0.389**	0.105
Deadeners	0.039**	0.013	-0.218	0.168
Heavyweights	0.100**	0.013	-0.280	0.173
Age*Abstainers			0.029**	0.007
Age*Dabblers			0.017*	0.007
Age*Deadeners			0.016	0.011
Age*Heavyweights			0.024*	0.011
Pearson R^2	0.133		0.135	
n=17,429				
**p<0.01 *p<0.05				

TABLE 37: Binary Logistic Regression Predicting Self-Report Criminal Versatility

Dependent Variable: Self-Report Criminal Versatility
Omitted Cluster: Deadeners

	Set 1		Set 2	
	b	SE	b	SE
Constant	0.437**	0.018	0.569**	0.134
Age	-0.010**	0.001	-0.018*	0.009
Gender (male=1)	0.045**	0.003	0.044**	0.003
Income Help	0.029**	0.004	0.028**	0.004
African-American	0.050**	0.004	0.049**	0.004
Native American	0.041**	0.012	0.041**	0.012
Asian-American	-0.011	0.028	-0.012	0.008
Multiple Race	0.028**	0.011	0.027*	0.011
Hispanic	0.022**	0.004	0.022**	0.004
Abstainers	-0.251**	0.010	-0.444**	0.135
Dabblers	-0.161**	0.010	-0.171	0.136
Benders	-0.039**	0.013	0.218	0.168
Heavyweights	0.061**	0.014	-0.062	0.194
Age*Abstainers			0.013	0.009
Age*Dabblers			0.000	0.009
Age*Benders			-0.016	0.011
Age*Heavyweights			0.008	0.012
Pearson R^2	0.133		0.135	
n=17,429				
**p<0.01 *p<0.05				

TABLE 38: Binary Logistic Regression Predicting Self-Report Criminal Versatility

Dependent Variable: Self-Report Criminal Versatility
Omitted Cluster: Heavyweights

	Set 1		Set 2	
	b	SE	b	SE
Constant	0.498**	0.018	0.507**	0.140
Age	-0.010**	0.001	-0.010	0.009
Gender (male=1)	0.045**	0.003	0.044**	0.003
Income Help	0.029**	0.004	0.028**	0.004
African-American	0.050**	0.004	0.049**	0.004
Native American	0.041**	0.012	0.041**	0.012
Asian-American	-0.011	0.028	-0.012	0.008
Multiple Race	0.028**	0.011	0.027*	0.011
Hispanic	0.022**	0.004	0.022**	0.004
Abstainers	-0.312**	0.010	-0.382**	0.141
Dabblers	-0.222**	0.010	-0.109	0.142
Benders	-0.100**	0.013	0.280	0.173
Deadeners	-0.061**	0.014	0.062	0.194
Age*Abstainers			0.005	0.009
Age*Dabblers			-0.008	0.009
Age*Benders			-0.024*	0.011
Age*Deadeners			-0.008	0.012
Pearson R^2	0.133		0.135	
n=17,429				
**p<0.01 *p<0.05				

Appendix F: Tukey's Honest Significant Test

TABLE 39: Tukey's HST between Clusters and Traditional Measures					
Varibale	Abstainers Dabblers	Benders	Deadeners Heavies		Total
Alcohol (D)	0.000a 0.869b	0.993c	0.897b	0.930b	0.342^
Marijuana (D)	0.000a 0.303b	0.549c	0.929d	1.000e	0.152
Cocaine (D)	0.000a 0.012b	0.070c	0.194d	0.282e	0.016
Crack (D)	0.000a 0.015a	0.015b	0.071c	0.067c	0.004
Heroin (D)	0.000a 0.002b	0.009c	0.034d	0.030d	0.002
Inhalants (D)	0.000a 0.082b	0.110c	0.160d	0.177d	0.036
Pain Relievers (D)	0.000a 0.132b	0.239c	0.365d	0.424e	0.065
Hallucinogens (D)	0.000a 0.059b	0.213c	0.365d	0.480e	0.043
Tranquilizers (D)	0.000a 0.023b	0.095c	0.128d	0.215e	0.018
Stimulants (D)	0.000a 0.036b	0.094c	0.140d	0.274e	0.023
Sedatives (D)	0.000a 0.009b	0.017b	0.026c	0.043d	0.005
Meth. (D)	0.000a 0.010b	0.035c	0.054d	0.126e	0.008
Alcohol (O)	0.000a 1.213b	3.585c	2.336d	2.603e	0.596
Marijuana (O)	0.000a 0.480b	1.092c	3.336d	3.989e	0.343
Cocaine (O)	0.000a 0.018b	0.094c	0.425d	0.461d	0.027
Crack (O)	0.000a 0.002a	0.020b	0.160c	0.105d	0.007
Heroin (O)	0.000a 0.003a	0.011a	0.063b	0.059b	0.004^^
Inhalants (O)	0.000a 0.125b	0.174c	0.245d	0.276d	0.055
Pain Relievers (O)	0.000a 0.221b	0.422c	0.875d	0.729e	0.116
Hallucinogens (O)	0.000a 0.072b	0.398c	0.553d	0.812e	0.064
Tranquilizers (O)	0.000a 0.033b	0.200c	0.217c	0.391d	0.029
Stimulants (O)	0.000a 0.064b	0.154c	0.242d	0.649e	0.044
Sedatives (O)	0.000a 0.016b	0.029b	0.057c	0.097d	0.009
Meth (O)	0.000a 0.014b	0.051c	0.080d	0.306e	0.014
Overall Drug (D)	0.000a 1.000b	1.000b	1.000b	1.000b	0.387
Overall Drug (O)	0.000a 1.704b	3.853c	4.000d	4.000d	0.821
Sum Drug (D)	0.000a 1.539b	2.437c	3.362d	4.046e	0.713
Sum Drug (O)	0.000a 2.262b	6.231c	8.855d	10.477e	1.307
Guttman Scale	0.000a 1.428b	1.976c	2.476d	2.641e	0.616

n=17,429   D=dichotomous O=ordinal
^Heavyweights and Dabblers are significantly different from one another
^^Benders and Abstainers are significantly different from one another
Note-Letters after each coefficient designate statistical similarities (if the letter is the same) or differences (if the letter is different) from the other clusters.

Appendix G: Background Variables Predicting Traditional Substance Use Measures

TABLE 40: Binary Logistic Regression of Background Variables Predicting Dichotomous Measures of Drug Use

Dep V	Alcohol	Marijuana	Cocaine	Crack	Heroin	Inhalant
Age	0.548**	0.547**	0.615**	0.593**	0.359**	0.032
Gender	-0.140**	-0.081	-0.025	-0.264	-0.523	-0.147
Inc Sub	0.022	0.199**	0.050	0.409	0.413	0.094
Afr-A	-0.743**	-0.357**	-1.984**	-2.432*	-15.500	-0.883**
Native	-0.073	0.627**	0.929**	1.024	-15.570	-0.119
Asi-A	-0.895**	-1.013**	-1.736*	-1.032	-0.660	-0.271
Multi	-0.149	-0.138	0.195	-15.751	0.581	0.314
Hisp	-0.275**	-0.205*	-0.059	-0.371	-15.459	-0.105

Dep V	Pain Rel.	Hallucin.	Tranq.	Stimulant	Sedative	Meth.
Age	0.285**	0.470**	0.432**	0.339**	0.179**	0.405**
Gender	-0.251**	-0.164*	-0.254*	-0.414**	-0.580*	-0.528**
Inc Sub	0.272**	0.218*	0.312*	0.267*	-0.449	0.185
Afr-A	-0.319**	-1.280**	-1.712**	-1.019**	0.291	-0.991**
Native	0.197	0.343	-0.319	0.413	-0.224	0.635
Asi-A	-0.657**	-0.503*	-0.991*	-0.830*	-1.002	-0.572
Multi	0.260	0.050	0.067	0.095	0.235	-0.014
Hisp	-0.239*	-0.635**	-0.799**	-0.469**	-0.432	-0.271

n=17,429
**p<0.01   *p<0.05

TABLE 41: Ordered Logit Regression of Background Variables Predicting Ordinal Measures of Drug Use

Dep V	Alcohol	Marijuana	Cocaine	Crack	Heroin	Inhalant
Age	0.548**	0.546**	0.616**	0.593**	0.359**	0.030
Gender	-0.087**	0.113*	-0.027	-0.264	-0.522	-0.148
Inc Sub	0.051	0.220**	0.049	0.413	0.410	0.095
Afr-A	-0.714**	-0.354**	-1.982**	-2.433*	-19.219	-0.880**
Native	-0.012	0.699**	0.937**	1.031	-19.296	-0.120
Asi-A	-0.913**	-1.014**	-1.735*	-1.034*	-0.659	-0.270
Multi	-0.090	0.161	-0.191	-18.879	0.577	0.317
Hisp	-0.243**	-0.186**	-0.058	-0.371	-19.173	-0.105

Dep V	Pain Rel.	Hallucin.	Tranq.	Stimulant	Sedative	Meth.
Age	0.282**	0.469**	0.432**	0.339**	0.179**	0.405**
Gender	-0.252**	-0.158*	-0.252*	-0.415*	-0.580*	-0.530**
Inc Sub	0.284**	0.217*	0.316*	0.265*	-0.449	0.183
Afr-A	-0.318**	-1.277**	-1.711**	-1.020**	0.293	-0.991**
Native	0.203	0.349	-0.309	0.417	-0.222	0.638
Asi-A	-0.660**	-0.495*	-0.991*	-0.831*	-1.002	-0.568
Multi	0.243	0.053	0.065	0.087	0.237	-0.016
Hisp	-0.232*	-0.635**	-0.801**	-0.465**	-0.431	-0.270

n=17,429
**p<0.01   *p<0.05

TABLE 42: Multi-Nomial Logistic Regression, Binary Logistic Regression, and Ordered Logit Regression of Background Variables Predicting Drug Use Clusters and Overall Drug Use Measures

	ODich^^	OOrd^^^	SDich^^	SOrd^^^	Gutt^^
Age	0.505**	0.498**	0.050**	0.068**	0.503**
Gender	-0.110**	-0.048	-0.012**	-0.008	-0.094**
Inc Sub	0.076	0.133**	0.012**	0.023**	0.108**
Afr-A	-0.497**	-0.465**	-0.056**	-0.066**	-0.533**
Native	0.095	-0.217	0.027*	0.050**	0.239*
Asi-A	-0.762**	-0.788**	-0.077**	-0.106**	-0.814**
Multi	-0.075	-0.016	-0.001	0.003	-0.030
Hisp	-0.163**	-0.136**	-0.023**	-0.022**	-0.193**

	Abst v Dab^	Abst v Bend^	Abst v Deaden^	Abst v Heavies^
Age	0.457**	0.756**	0.699**	0.824**
Gender	-0.161**	-0.043	0.126	0.460**
Inc Sub	0.040	0.193	0.256	0.320
Afr-A	-0.477**	-0.701**	-0.414*	-0.638**
Native	-0.012	-0.310	0.996*	0.710*
Asi-A	-0.675**	-0.927**	-1.749**	-1.629**
Multi	-0.119	-0.277	0.161	0.540
Hisp	-0.171**	-0.271*	-0.117	-0.193

n=17,429

**$p<0.01$ *$p<0.05$

^ Multi-Nomial Logistic Regression (Abstainers are Omitted Category)

^^ Binary Logistic Regression

^^^ Ordered Logit Regression

Appendix H: Background Variables and Traditional Measures of
Substance Use Predicting Criminal Behavior

**TABLE 43: Binary Logistic Regression and Ordinary Least
Squares Regression of Individual Dichotomous Drug Use
Measures Predicting Self-Report Measures of Crime**

DV >	Crime^	Arrests^	Versatility^^
Alcohol (Dichotomous)	0.661**	0.870**	0.060**
Marijuana (Dichotomous)	0.591**	1.044**	0.073**
Cocaine (Dichotomous)	0.576**	0.554**	0.080**
Crack (Dichotomous)	-0.295	0.055	-0.028*
Heroin (Dichotomous)	0.049	0.260	0.073*
Inhalant (Dichotomous)	0.842**	0.271	0.085**
Pain Reliever (Dich)	0.335**	0.249	0.040**
Hallucinogen (Dichotomous)	0.472**	0.561**	0.070**
Tranquilizer (Dichotomous)	0.099	-0.171	0.014
Stimulant (Dichotomous)	0.657**	0.653**	0.065**
Sedative (Dichotomous)	0.562*	0.377	0.071
Methamphetamines (Dich)	0.194	-0.004	-0.018

n=17,429
**p<0.01 *p<0.05
^Binary Logistic Regression
^^Ordinary Least Squares Regression

TABLE 44: Binary Logistic Regression and Ordinary Least Squares Regression of Individual Ordinal Drug Use Measures Predicting Self-Report Measures of Crime

Dependent Variable >	Crime^	Arrests^	Versatility^^
Alcohol (Ordinal)	1.742**	1.847**	0.170**
Marijuana (Ordinal)	1.155**	1.899**	0.152**
Cocaine (Ordinal)	0.920	1.075*	0.144**
Crack (Ordinal)	-1.445	-0.313	-0.172
Heroin (Ordinal)	0.218	0.144	0.176*
Inhalant (Ordinal)	2.132**	0.597	0.202**
Pain Reliever (Ordinal)	0.669**	0.395	0.080**
Hallucinogen (Ordinal)	0.846**	0.970**	0.129**
Tranquilizer (Ordinal)	-0.203	-0.443	0.020
Stimulant (Ordinal)	1.266**	0.966*	0.113**
Sedative (Ordinal)	0.930	0.107	0.087**
Methamphetamine (Ordinal)	0.708	-0.082	0.071

n=17,429
**p<0.01 *p<0.05
^Binary Logistic Regression
^^Ordinary Least Squares Regression

TABLE 45: Binary Logistic Regression and Ordinary Least Squares Regression of Cluster and Overall Drug Use Measures Predicting Self-Report Measures of Crime

Dependent Variable >	Crime^	Arrests^	Versatility^^
Overall Drug Use (Dichotomous)	1.123**	1.738**	0.117**
Overall Drug Use (Ordinal)	2.676**	3.727**	0.293**
Sum of Dichotomous (Ordinal)	2.910**	3.998**	0.324**
Sum or Ordinal (Ordinal)	2.206**	2.843**	0.250**
Guttman Scale (Ordinal)	3.078**	4.593**	0.336**
Dabblers (Abs Omitted)	0.945**	1.410**	0.090**
Benders (Abs Omitted)	1.799**	2.311**	0.212**
Deadeners (Abs Omitted)	2.129**	2.694**	0.251**
Heavies (Abs Omitted)	2.409**	3.027**	0.312**

n=17,429
**p<0.01   *p<0.05
^Binary Logistic Regression
^^Ordinary Least Squares Regression

Appendix I: University of Nebraska-Lincoln Research Protocol

The University of Nebraska-Lincoln requires that all research receive approval for project research from the Institutional Review Board (IRB). The 2001 National Household Survey on Drug Abuse was used, which has a sample of 17,429 adolescents. This study utilized secondary data analysis, which puts participants at "less than minimal risk." The data were obtained through the Inter-university Consortium for Political and Social Research (ICPSR) at the University of Michigan (data #3580). IRB approval was applied for on December of 2003 approval received on February 18, 2004. In the approval letter, the IRB committee stated, "Your proposal seems to be in compliance with this institution's Federal Wide Assurance 00002258 and the DHHS Regulations for the Protection of Human Subjects (45 CFR 46) and has been classified as exempt."

IRB#: 2004-02-169 EX.

Reseasrch Compliance Services
University of Nebraska-Lincoln
Alexander Building West
312 North 14th Street
PO Box 880415
Lincoln, NE 68588-0415

References

Akers, Ronald L. and John K. Cochran. (1985). "Adolescent Marijuana Use: A Test of Three Theories of Deviant Behavior." *Deviant Behavior*, 6, 323-346.

Akers, Ronald L. and Gang Lee. (1998). "Age, Social Learning, and Social Bonding in Adolescent Substance Use." *Deviant Behavior*, 20, 1-25.

Aldenderfer, Mark S. and Roger K. Blashfield. (1984). "Cluster Analysis." *Quantitative Applications in the Social Sciences*. Michael S. Lewis-Beck, ed. Newbury Park: Sage.

Altschuler, David M. and Paul J. Brounstein. (1991). "Patterns of Drug Use, Drug Trafficking, and Other Delinquency Among Inner-City Adolescent Males in Washington, D.C." *Criminology*, 29, 589-622.

Andrews, Judy A., Hyman Hops, and Susan C. Duncan. (1997). "Adolescent Columning of Parent Substance Use: The Moderating Effect of the Relationship with the Parent." *Journal of Family Psychology*, 11, 259-270.

Arafat, Ibtihaj. (1979). "Drinking Behavior in High School, College, and Adult Groups." *Free Inquiry in Creative Sociology*, 7, 87-91.

Bahr, Steohen J., Suzanne L. Maughan, Anastasios C. Marcos, and Bingdao Li. (1998). "Family, Religiosity, and the Risk of Adolescent Drug Use." *Journal of Marriage and the Family*, 60, 979-992.

Barrera, Jr., Manuel, Anthony Biglan, Dennis Ary, and Fuzhong Li. (2001). "Replication of a Problem Behavior Column with American Indian, Hispanic, and Caucasian Youth." *Journal of Early Adolescence*, 21, 133-157.

Bean, Phillip. (2002). *Drugs and Crime*. Portland: Willian.

Benda, Brent B. (1995). "The Effect of Religion on Adolescent Delinquency Revisited." *Journal of Research in Crime and Delinquency*, 32, 446-466.

Bensley, Lillian Southwick, Susan J. Spieker, Juliet van Eenwyk, and Judy Schoder. (1999). "Self-Report Abuse History and Adolescent Problem Behaviors. II. Alcohol and Drug Use." *Journal of Adolescent Health*, 24, 173-180.

Beyers, Jennifer M. and Rolf Loeber. (2003). "Untangling Developmental Relations Between Depressed Mood and Delinquency in Male Adolescents." *Journal of Abnormal Child Psychology*, 31, 247-266.

Blumstein, Alfred and Jacqueline Cohen. (1987). "Characterizing Criminal Careers." *Science*, 237, 985-991.

Britt, Chester L. (1994). "Versatility." *The General Theory of Deviance*. Travis Hirschi and Michael Gottfredson, eds. New Brunswick: Transaction.

Brown, Tamara L., Gregory S. Parks, Rick S. Zimmerman, and Clarenda M. Phillips. (2001). "The Role of Religion in Predicting Adolescent Alcohol Use and Problem Drinking." Journal of Studies on Alcohol, 62, 696-705.

Brownfield, David and Ann Marie Sorenson. (1991). "Religion and Drug Use Among Adolescents: a Social Support Conceptualization and Interpretation." *Deviant Behavior*, 12, 259-276

Carmines, Edward G. and Richard A. Zeller. (1979). "Reliability and Validity Assesment." *Quantitative Applications in the Social Sciences*. Michael S. Lewis-Beck, ed. Newbury Park: Sage.

Chapple, Constance L, Trina L. Hope, and Scott W. Whiteford. (2005). "Parenting, Self-Control, and Adolescent Substance Use: a Longitudinal Analysis." *Journal of Child and Adolescent Substance Use.*

Cochran, John K. (1993). "The Variable Effects of Religiosity and Denomination on Adolescent Self-Reported Alcohol Use by Beverage Type." *Journal of Drug Issues*, 23, 479-491.

Cochran, John K. and Ronald L. Akers. (1989). "Beyond Hellfire: An Exploration of the Variable Effects of Religiosity on Adolescent Marijuana and Alcohol Use." *Journal of Research in Crime and Delinquency*, 26, 198-225.

Darlington, Richard B. (1990). *Regression and Linear Columns*. San Francisco: McGraw-Hill.

Dawkins, Marvin P. (1997). "Drug Use and Violent Crime Among Adolescents." *Adolescence*, 32, 395-404

DeMaris, Alfred. 1995. "A Tutorial in Logistic Regression." *Journal of Marriage and the Family*, 57, 956-968.

DeVellis, Robert F. (1991). *Scale Development: Theory and Applications.* Newbury Park: Sage.

Diego, Miguel A., Tiffany M. Field, and Christopher E. Sanders. (2003). *Adolescence*, 38, 35-42.

Dillman, Don A. (2000). *Mail and Internet Surveys: The Tailored Design Method.* 2nd ed. New York: John Wiley & Sons.

Donnermeyer, Joseph F. (1993). "Rural Youth Usage of Alcohol, Marijuana, and 'Hard' Drugs." *The International Journal of the Addictions*, 28, 249-255.

Downs, William R. and Joan F. Robertson. (1990). "Referral for Treatment Among Adolescent Alcohol and Drug Abusers." *Journal of Research in Crime and Delinquency*, 27, 190-209.

Duncan, Terry E., Elizabeth Tildesley, Susan C. Duncan, and Hyman Hops. (1995). "The Consistency of Family and Peer Influences on the Development of Substance Use in Adolescence." *Addiction*, 1995, 1647-1660.

Ellickson, Phyllis, Khanh Bui, Robert Bell, and Kimberly A. McGuigan. (1998). "Does Early Drug Use Increase the Risk of Dropping out of High School?" Journal *of Drug Issues*, 28, 357-380.

Fagan, Jeffrey, Joseph G. Weis, and Yu-The Cheng. (1990). "Delinquency and Substance Use Among Inner-City Students. *Journal of Drug Issues*, 20, 351-402.

Flannery, Daniel J., Laura L. Williams, Alexander T. Vazsonyi. (1999). "Who Are They with and What are They Doing? Delinquent Behavior, Substance Use, and Early Adolescents' After-School Time." *American Journal of Orthopsychiatry*, 69, 247-253.

Fox, John. (1991). "Regression Diagnostics." *Quantitative Applications in the Social Sciences.* Michael S. Lewis-Beck, ed. Newbury Park: Sage.

Fox, John. (1997). *Applied Regression Analysis, Linear Columns, and Related Methods.* Thousand Oaks: Sage.

Ford, Jason A. (2005). "The Connection between Heavy Drinking and Juvenile Delinquency during Adolescence." *Sociological Spectrum*, 25, 629-650.

Goode, Erich. (2001). "Drug Use in America: An Overview." *Readings in Deviant Behavior.* Alex Thio and Thomas Calhoun, eds. 2nd edition. New York: Allyn and Bacon.

Gottfredson, Michael and Travis Hirschi. (1990). *General Theory of Crime.* Stanford: Stanford Press.

Graham, Nanette. (1996). "The Influence of Predictors on Adolescent Drug Use." *Youth and Society*, 28, 215-235.

Grella, Christine E., Shama Chaiken, and M. Douglass Anglin. (1995). "Procedure fro Assessing the Validity of Self-Report Data on High-Risk Sex Behaviors from Heroin Addicts Entering Free Methadone Treatment." *Journal of Drug Issues*, 25, 723-733.

Harrison, Patricia A., Jayne A. Fulkerson, and Timothy J. Beebe. (1997). "Multiple Substance Use Among Adolescent Physical and Sexual Abuse Victims." *Child Abuse and Neglect*, 21, 529-539.

Havey, J. Michael and David K. Dodd. (1994). "Children of Alcoholics, Negative Life Events, and Early Experimentation with Drugs." *Journal of School Psychology*, 33, 305-317.

Heimer, Karen (1997). "Socio-economic Status, Subcultural Definitions and Violent Delinquency." *Social Forces*, 75, 779-833.

Hindelang, Michael. (1979). "Sex Differences in Criminal Activity." *Social Problems,* 27, 143-156.

Hirschi, Travis. (1969). *The Causes of Delinquency.* Berkeley: University of California Press.

Hirschi, Travis, and Michael Gottfredson. (1983). "Age and the Explanation of Crime." *American Journal of Sociology*, 89, 552-584.

Hoaglin, David C., Frederick Mosteller, and John W. Tukey. (1983). *Understanding Robust and Exploratory Data Analysis.* New York: Wiley.

Hundleby, John D. and G. William Mercer. (1987). "Family and Friends as Social Environments and Their Relationship to Young Adolescents' Use of Alcohol, Tobacco, and Marijuana. *Journal of Marriage of the Family*, 49, 151-164.

Jobling, D. and E.J. Snell. (1961). "The Use of the Coefficient of Reproducibility in Attitude Scaling." *The Incorporated Statistician*, 11, 110-118.

Kandel, Denise. (1975). "Stages in Adolescent Involvement in Drug Use." *Science*, 190, 912-914.

Kandel, Denise B., Kazuo Yamaguchi, and Kevin Chien. (1992). "Stages of Progression in Drug Involvement from Adolescence to Adulthood: Further Evidence for the Gateway Theory." *Journal of Studies on Alcohol*, 53, 447-457.

Keller, Thomas E., Richard F. Catalano, Kevin P. Haggerty, and Charles B. Fleming. (2002). "Parent Figure Transitions and Delinquency and Drug Use Among Early Adolescent Children of Substance Abusers." *American Journal of Drug and Alcohol Abuse*, 28, 399-427.

Kelly, Kathleen J., Maria Leonora G. Comello, and Liza C.P. Hunn. (2002). "Parent-Child Communication, Perceived Sanctions Against Drug Use, and Youth Drug Involvement." *Adolescence*, 37, 775-787.

Kinnier, Richard T., Arlene T. Metha, Jeffrey L. Okey, and Jeanmarie Keim. (1994). "Adolescent Substance Abuse and Psychological Health. *Journal of Alcohol and Drug Education*, 40, 51-56.

Klein, Malcolm W. (1984). "Offense Specialists and Versatility Among Juveniles. *British Journal of Criminology*, 24, 185-194.

Klein, Malcolm W. (1995). *The American Street Gang*. New York: Oxford.

Kline, Rex B. (1998). *Principles and Practice of Structural Equation Columning*. New York: Guilford Press.

Lempers, Jacques D., Diana Clark-Lempers, and Ronald L. Simmons. (1989). "Economic Hardship, Parenting, and Distress in Adolescence." *Child Development*, 60, 25-39.

Lewis-Beck, Michael S. (1980). "Applied Regression: An Introduction." *Quantitative Applications in the Social Sciences*. Michael S. Lewis-Beck, ed. Newbury Park: Sage.

Long, J. Scott. (1997). *Regression Columns for Categorical and Limited Dependant Variables*. Thousand Oaks: Sage.

Marcos, Anastasios, Stephen J. Bahr, and Richard E. Johnson. (1986). "Test of a Bonding/Association Theory of Adolescent Drug Use." *Social Forces*, 65, 135-161.

Matsueda, Ross L. and Karen Heimer. (1987). "Race, Family Structure, and Delinquency: A Test of Differential Association and Social Control Theories." *American Sociological Review,* 52, 826-840.

McBride, Anthony A., George W. Joe, and D. Dwayne Simpson. (1991). "Prediction of Long-Term Alcohol Use, Drug Use, and Criminality Among Inhalant Users." *Hispanic Journal of Behavioral Sciences,* 13, 315-323.

McGee, Zina T. (1992). "Social Class Differences in Parental and Peer Influence on Adolescent Drug Use." *Deviant Behavior*, 13, 349-372.

McIver, John P. and Carmines, Edward G. (1981). *Unidimensional Scaling*. Beverly Hills: Sage.

Miller-Johnson, Shari, John E. Lochman, John D. Cole, Robert Terry, and Clarine Hyman. (1998). "Co-morbidity of Conduct and Depressive Problems at Sixth Grade: Substance Use Outcomes Across Adolescence." *Journal of Abnormal Child Psychology*, 26, 221-232.

Moffitt, Terrie E. (1993). "Adolescence-Limited and Life-Course-Persistent Antisocial Behavior: A Developmental Taxonomy." *Psychological Review*, 100, 674-701.

Moffitt, Terrie E. (1997). "Adolescence-Limited and Life-Course-Persistent Offending: A Complementary Pair of Developmental Theories." *Developmental Theories of Crime and Delinquency*. Terrance Thornberry, ed. 11-54.

Muthen, Bengt and Linda K. Muthen. (2000). "Integrating Person-Centered and Variable-Centered Analysis: Growth Mixture Modeling with Latent Trajectory Classes." *Alcoholism: Clinical and Experimental Research*, 24, 882-891.

Novins, Douglas K. and Christina M. Mitchell. (1998). "Factors Associated with Marijuana Use among American Indian Adolescents." *Addiction*, 93, 1963-1702.

Nunnally, Jum C. and Ira H. Bernstein. (1994). *Psychometric Theory*. 3rd. ed. San Francisco: McGraw Hill.

Osgood, D. Wayne, Janet K. Wilson, Patrick M. O'Malley, Jerald G. Bachman, Lloyd D. Johnston. (1996). "Routine Activities and Individual Deviant Behavior." *American Sociological Review*, 61, 635-655.

Parker, Keith D., Thomas Calhoun, and Greg Weaver. (2000). "Variables Associated with Adolescent Alcohol Use: A Multiethnic Comparison." *Journal of Social Psychology*, 140, 51-62.

Parker, Keith D., Greg Weaver, and Thomas Calhoun. (1995). "Predictors of Alcohol and Drug Use: A Multi-ethnic Comparison." *The Journal of Social-Psychology*, 135, 581-590.

Robinson, John P. (1973). "Toward a More Appropriate Use of Guttman Scaling." *The Public Opinion Quarterly*, 37, 260-267.

Sampson, Robert J. and John H. Laub. (2003). "Life-Course Desisters? Trajectories of Crime Among Delinquent Boys Followed to Age 70." *Criminology*, 41, 555-592.

Schroeder, Larry D., David L. Sjoquist, and Paula E. Stephan. (1986). "Understanding Regression Analysis: An Introductory Guide." *Quantitative Applications in the Social Sciences.* Michael S. Lewis-Beck, ed. Newbury Park: Sage.

Shaw, Clifford, and Henry McKay. (1942). *Juvenile Delinquency and Urban Areas.* Chicago: University of Chicago Press.

Simons-Morton, Bruce and Ruran S. Chen. (2006). "Over Time Relationships between Early Adolescent and Peer Substance Use." *Addictive Behaviors,* 31, 1211-1223.

Smart, Laura S., Thomas R. Chibucos, and Larry A. Didier. (1990). "Adolescent Substance Use and Perceived Family Functioning." *Journal of Family Issues,* 11, 208-227.

Sokol-Katz, Jan, Roger Dunham, and Rick Zimmerman. (1997). "Family Structure versus Parental Attachment in Controlling Adolescent Deviant Behavior: A Social Control Column." *Adolescence,* 32, 199-215.

Sommers, Ira and Deborah R. Baskin. (1993). "Situational Context of Violent Female offending." *Journal of Research in Crime and Delinquency,* 30, 136-162.

Statistical Package for the Social Sciences 11.5 (SPSS). (2003). *Advanced Columns.* Chicago: SPSS.

Stice, Eric and Manuel Barrera, Jr. (1995). "A Longitudinal Examination of the Reciprocal Relations Between Perceived Parenting and Adolescents' Substance Use and Externalizing Behaviors." *Developmental Psychology,* 31, 322-334.

Stice, Eric and Manuel Barrera, Jr., and Laurie Chassin. (1993). "Relation of Parental Support and Control to Adolescents' Externalizing Symptomatology and Substance Use: A Longitudinal Examination of Curvilinear Effects." Journal *of Abnormal Child Psychology,* 21, 609-629.

Swaim, Randall C., Scott C. Bates, and Ernest L. Chavez. (1998). "Structural Equation Socialization Column of Substance Use among Mexican-American and White Non-Hispanic School Dropouts." *Journal of Adolescent Health,* 23, 128-138.

Tibachnick, Barbara G. and Linda S. Fidell. (1996). *Using Multivariate Statistics.* 3rd. ed. New York: Harper Collins.

Thompson, William E., Jim Mitchell, and Richard A. Dodder. (1984). "An Empirical Test of Hirschi's Control Theory of Delinquency." *Deviant Behavior,* 5, 11-22.

Thornberry, Terence P., Marvin D. Krohn, Alan J. Lizotte, and Deborah Chard-Wierschiem. (1993). "The Role of Juvenile Gangs in Facilitating Delinquent Behavior." *Journal of Research in Crime and Delinquency.* (30): 55-87.

U.S. Dept. of Health and Human Services, Substance Abuse and Mental Health Services Administration, Office of Applied Studies. NATIONAL HOUSEHOLD SURVEY ON DRUG ABUSE, 2001 [Computer File]. ICPSR version. Research Triangle Park, NC: Research Triangle Institute [producer], 2002. Ann Arbor, MI: Inter-University Consortium for Political and Social Research [distributor], 2003.

Ward, James. (1963). "Hierarchical Grouping to Optimize an Objective Function." *Journal of the American Statistical Association,* 58, 236-244.

Warr, Mark. (1993). "Age, Peers, and Delinquency." *Criminology,* 31, 17-40.

Wechsler, Henry and Denise Thum. (1973). "Teen-Age Drinking, Drug Use, and Social Correlates." *Quarterly Journal of Studies on Alcohol,* 34, 1220-1227.

Welte, John W. and Grace M. Barnes. (1985). "Alcohol: The Gateway to Other Drug Use Among Secondary-School Students." *Journal of Youth and Adolescence,* 14, 487-499.

Welte, John W., Lening Zhang, and William F. Wieczorek. (2001). "The Effects of Substance Use on Specific Types of Criminal Offending in Young Men." *Journal of Research in Crime and Delinquency,* 38, 416-438.

Welte, John W., Grace M. Barnes, Joseph H. Hoffman, William F. Wieczorek, and Lening Zhang. (2005). "Substance Involvement and the Trajectory of Criminal Offending in Young Males." *The American Journal of Drug and Alcohol Abuse,* 31, 267-284.

White, Helene Raskin, Valerie Johnson, Carole Gozansky Garrison. (1985). "The Drug-Crime Nexus Among Adolescents and Their Peers." *Deviant Behavior,* 6, 183-204.

Whiteford, Scott W. (2004). A Cluster-Analytic of *Adolescent Substance Use: Investigating the Drug-Crime Relationship.* Dissertation: University of Nebraska-Lincoln.

Widom, Cathy Spatz. (1989). "Could Abuse, Neglect, and Violent Criminal Behavior." *Criminology,* 27, 251-271.

Wilsnack, Richard W. and Sharon C. Wilsnack. 1980. "Drinking and Denial of Social Obligations among Adolescent Boys." *Journal of Studies on Alcohol.* (41): 1118-1133.

Wood, Peter B., John K. Cochran, Betty Pfefferbaum, and Bruce J. Arneklev. (1995). "Sensation-Seeking and Delinquent Substance Use: An Extension of Learning Theory." *The Journal of Drug Issues*, 25, 173-193.

Youniss, James, Miranda Yates, and Yang Su. (1997). "Social Integration: Community Service and Marijuana Use in High School Seniors. *Journal of Adolescent Research*, 12, 245-262.

Index